Practicing Stillness

PRACTICING
STILLNESS

50 Simple Exercises to Slow Down, Live in the Moment, and Find Peace

Nissa Keyashian, MD

ROCKRIDGE
PRESS

First Rockridge Press trade paperback edition 2022

Rockridge Press and the Rockridge Press logo are trademarks or registered trademarks of Callisto Media Inc. and/or its affiliates in the United States and other countries and may not be used without written permission.

For general information on our other products and services, please contact our Customer Care Department within the United States at (866) 744-2665, or outside the United States at (510) 253-0500.

Paperback ISBN: 978-1-63807-798-5
eBook ISBN: 978-1-68539-135-5

Manufactured in the United States of America

Interior and Cover Designer: Mando Daniel
Art Producer: Maya Melenchuk
Editor: Chloe Moffett
Production Manager: Martin Worthington

Author photo courtesy of Andrew Barrios

10 9 8 7 6 5 4 3 2 1 0

To my sons, Jack and River,
my inspiration for peace.

Contents

Introduction ix

How to Use This Book xi

Part One: An Introduction to Stillness 1

Chapter 1: Stillness 101 3

A Brief History of Stillness Practices 3
Stillness Practices Today 6
What I Mean by Stillness 7
The Benefits of a Stillness Practice 9

Chapter 2: Building a Stillness Practice 15

The Aspects of Stillness 15
Building a Practice 18
What to Expect 21
Your Stillness Toolbox 23
Keeping a Beginner's Mind 24

Part Two: 50 Practices for Stillness 29

Mindfulness of the Breath 30
Awareness of Sense Perceptions 32
Introduction to Mindful Movement 34
Calm Breathing 36
Body Scan 38
Walking Meditation 40
Loving-Kindness Meditation 42
Awareness of Thoughts 44
Releasing Tension in the Head and Neck 46
Journaling 48

The Seven Principles of Mindfulness 50

Eating in Stillness 52

Releasing Tension in the Body 54

Mindful Morning Routine 56

Awareness of Emotions 58

Awareness of Ego 60

Mindful Bathing 62

Awareness of Aversion 64

Stillness before Sleep 66

Awareness of Craving 68

Warming Up the Spine 70

Awareness of Confusion 72

Stillness before Responding to Emails 74

Mindfulness in Household Chores 76

Self-Compassion with Difficult Emotions 78

Stillness in Relationships 80

Street Loving-Kindness Meditation 82

Awareness of Fear 84

Stillness on the Go 86

Awareness of Anger 88

Sun Salutation 90

Awareness of Sadness 92

Stillness with Children 94

Embracing Your Inner Child 96

Gratitude Practice 98

Stillness in Shopping 100

Work-Life Balance 102

Balancing Postures 104

Media Reflection 106

Hip Opening 108

Forgiveness Practice 110

Moving in the Direction of Love 112
Practicing with Conflict 114
Open Awareness 116
Awareness of Interdependence 118
Cultivating Contentment 120
Restorative Yoga 122
Living with Higher Purpose and
    Releasing Attachments 124
Balancing Growth and Acceptance 126
Accepting Impermanence 128

Moving Forward in Peace 131

Resources 132

References 134

Index 138

Introduction

Most of us want to see more peace in the world. Finding calm and stillness in yourself is the first step. You'll find stillness inside by being grounded in your body, bringing your attention to your sense perceptions, and building awareness about your thoughts and emotions. The practice of stillness teaches you to find the joy, love, and beauty that always exist in the present moment.

Practicing stillness also teaches you to show up for yourself and other people with love, kindness, and compassion. Suffering has always been a part of the human condition, but many of us wonder whether this suffering is growing worse with time.

Practicing stillness is a powerful way to alleviate this suffering.

My stillness practice flourished in 2008 during a very difficult time in my life. Although I originally went to medical school to become a psychiatrist, I got distracted along the way and decided to pursue internal medicine. Shortly after starting my residency, I was miserable and suffering and ended up leaving the program. For several months afterward, I struggled with anxiety and depression. Having just moved, purchased a home, and accumulated $200,000 in school loans, I was plagued by the idea that maybe I should never have gone to medical school in the first place.

During this very difficult time, I started reading about mindfulness and stillness and came across the seven principles of mindfulness: non-striving, non-judging, letting go, acceptance, patience, trust, and beginner's mind. These principles were almost in direct opposition to how I had been living most of my 27 years. But something deep down inside of me knew that practicing stillness and mindfulness was the key to rebalancing myself, and I have been practicing stillness ever since.

I made my way back home to psychiatry, and I learned how to incorporate mindfulness into the treatment I provide my patients. To this day, I find mindfulness to be one of the most powerful interventions I have to offer in my psychiatry practice.

I have found more peace in my heart—and in my relationships—as a result of my stillness practice, and I want to share this peace with you.

You may have found this book during a difficult time in your life. Perhaps you are suffering or feel deeply the suffering around you. No matter how unsteady it may feel, the ground is fertile for your stillness practice to blossom. This book will help you build a strong foundation of peace and stillness inside yourself that you can carry with you on your life journey.

Of course, like all worthwhile tasks, learning stillness takes time, intention, and practice, but I assure you that the investment is among the best you will make in this life. I am confident this book will help you reconnect to the stillness that embraces all of us.

The more peace we build in our hearts, the more we can improve our world.

How to Use This Book

This book is divided into two parts. Part 1 will introduce you to stillness, review the benefits of this practice, and provide you with a solid foundation on which you can build your own stillness practice. Part 2 is a list of 50 guided stillness practices.

In general, I recommend starting at the beginning and working your way to the end. If, along your journey, a particular stillness practice calls out to you, feel free to jump directly to that practice. This, after all, is your stillness journey, and trusting your inner wisdom will help you further deepen your practice.

Some of what you'll read here on stillness and the practices may feel different, weird, or even uncomfortable. Many of us have been conditioned to be constantly going, doing, and consuming and to tie our worth to these activities. Practicing stillness may initially feel very foreign and unnatural to you. But with continued practice, it will come more easily, and the benefits will be profound.

Also, please remember that the words in this book are merely signposts; the ultimate goal is to move past them into your direct experience of stillness.

PART ONE

An Introduction to Stillness

In this part, we'll take a deep dive into what stillness is and how it has been and can be practiced. The concept of stillness has been around for centuries, from the time of the Buddha's enlightenment all the way up to current clinical studies on the benefits of mindfulness. A rich stillness practice requires commitment and an understanding of the principles and tools of stillness. There are common obstacles, misconceptions, and frustrations in building a stillness practice, but these can all be overcome with patience and understanding of these challenges. As your stillness practice unfolds over time, you will begin to notice the benefits that come along with it. The information here will provide a foundation for the stillness practices in part 2.

CHAPTER 1

Stillness 101

Stillness has a long and rich history through the ages, beginning with the Buddha's teachings, and touching on the practice of yoga, stoicism, and the teachings of Jesus Christ, and moving right up to the present day. Today, more and more people are practicing stillness, and mindfulness and yoga have even found their way into childhood and adolescent education, life coaching, psychology, medicine, and other forms of psychotherapy.

I will share with you my personal practice of stillness and explain how I incorporate it into my professional practice. I will then dive deeper into what stillness means, its relevance in your busy and noisy world, and how the practice can enrich your life. There are many documented benefits of stillness for improving stress, anxiety, depression, physical health, and social well-being.

A Brief History of Stillness Practices

Whether in the context of religion, philosophy, education, health care, art, business, or other areas of life, people through many centuries, from many different backgrounds and cultures, have recognized how transformative stillness teachings and practices can be and have applied them to their lives in many ways.

Stillness is understood, taught, and practiced in Buddhism, yoga, stoicism, Christianity, and mindfulness practices, but this is not at all an exhaustive list. Stillness is practiced in many more religions, traditions, and cultures than I can mention in this book. You do not need to believe in a particular religion or subscribe to a certain philosophy to reap the benefits of stillness. My own stillness practice combines teachings and practices from a variety of belief systems and traditions.

Buddhism

Buddhism is the fourth-largest religion in the world and is based on the teachings of Gautama Buddha, who lived in ancient India probably in the sixth century BCE. The Buddha, which means the Enlightened One, taught about human suffering, the causes of suffering, the cessation of suffering, and the path that leads to the cessation of suffering. That path includes many teachings on stillness, in both formal meditation practice and mindfulness in day-to-day life.

Yoga

Yoga means "union" in Sanskrit—unifying body and mind, breath and energy, soul and body. It also comes from ancient India. Even though the word is often used to refer to a physical practice of specific poses, the physical practice (known as asanas) is only one of eight limbs of yoga. The remaining limbs are ethical standards, self-restraints and observances, breath control, turning inward, concentration, meditation, and absorption. The postures and the practice of ethical standards, breath control, and meditation are done in the service of stillness.

Stoicism

Stoicism is an ancient Greek philosophy that originated during the Hellenistic period in the third century BCE. Stoicism remained popular until the third century CE and has had several revivals, including most recently at the end of the twentieth century. Stoics such as Epictetus, who was born a slave, and Roman Emperor Marcus Aurelius believed people could achieve eudaimonia, or happiness, by living in accordance with nature and practicing the cardinal virtues of wisdom, courage, justice, and temperance. They recommended several spiritual exercises that promote stillness, including present-moment awareness, self-reflection, and equanimity, which means staying calm in difficult situations.

Christianity

Beginning in the second century CE and spanning all the way through to the present day, Christian mystics have engaged in spiritual practices that aim to still the mind to seek direct knowledge of and communion with God. These mystics pursue the threefold path of purification, illumination, and unification to transform their egoic self and ultimately live in harmony with God and all beings everywhere. Purification focuses on spiritual discipline, illumination refers to the Holy Spirit enlightening the mind, and unification is the experience of oneself as in some way united with God.

Mindfulness

Mindfulness is an ancient Buddhist teaching that is now taught and practiced in a variety of secular environments, including psychology, medicine, psychotherapy, life coaching, education, and business. Mindfulness is the practice of cultivating non-judgmental awareness of the present moment, including all your sensations, thoughts, and emotions. The seven principles of mindfulness are trust, letting go, acceptance, patience, non-striving, non-judging, and beginner's mind—a concept that encourages you to approach every moment as completely new, unique, and unlike any other moment. (When you have a deep mindfulness practice, you see that this really is true!) Mindfulness can be practiced formally, as in meditation, and informally in every moment of your life.

Stillness Practices Today

Stillness practices have been growing exponentially in recent times, likely because so many people have found them to be powerful healing tools as our lives become busier and noisier. Mindfulness and yoga have been studied scientifically and found to be helpful in treating many kinds of physical and mental health problems, including depression, anxiety, PTSD, and pain. Psychologists, physicians, psychotherapists, and life coaches are using stillness practices to bring healing to many of their patients and clients. Mindfulness and yoga are also being taught in broadening circles, from children to graduate students to seniors. Stillness and mindfulness have become part of many business training programs, as well.

I was first introduced to stillness practices through books and yoga classes. Some of my favorite American spiritual teachers, including Sharon Salzberg, Ram Dass, and Jack Kornfield, traveled to, studied, and practiced in Asia when they were young adults, then brought back the teachings they learned to the United States. Vietnamese Buddhist monk Thich Nhat Hanh was another powerful stillness teacher who joined with American Catholic mystic Thomas Merton and Martin Luther King Jr. to protest the Vietnam War. A few of my other favorite spiritual teachers include Marianne Williamson, Eckhart Tolle, Deepak Chopra, and Alan Watts. These teachers and many others have created books, websites, audio recordings, and podcasts that have transformed my stillness practice.

I meditate every morning for 30 minutes and practice yoga at least several times a week. Occasionally, I meditate for longer periods, and I have been on several silent retreats. I have also been on yoga retreats that incorporate chanting and breathwork. A powerful part of my stillness practice is working toward living in accordance with my values. The more I live in alignment with my values, the more stillness I find inside.

What I Mean by Stillness

We find stillness by fully inhabiting the present moment. When you are grounded deep into your body, feeling the movement of your breath or the contact your body makes with the surfaces around you, you come into stillness. You also generate stillness by becoming aware of your body and your breath as you move through space. As you build a more conscious awareness of your thoughts and emotions and reflect on your life and the ethical principles that you value most, you build clarity, strength of character, and peace of mind. Loving-kindness meditation allows you to cut through the fear and anger that plague so many people, and contemplative prayer allows you to rest in the love of others, of the world, of your spirituality.

We live in a loud and busy world that constantly demands so much from us. Stress and difficulty in our lives often feel inescapable, and if we are not mindful, the conflict in our outer world can produce turmoil within us. Stillness generates self-compassion—a powerful tool that carries us through difficult emotions.

The regular practice of stillness has transformed my life. Daily mindfulness, yoga, and spiritual practice have helped me create an enormous reserve of peace deep within myself that has made me a stronger and happier person. My relationships, my work as a psychiatrist, and my writing have all benefited greatly from this practice.

Creating stillness in your body, mind, and spirit builds a stronghold of calm deep within to help you weather the many storms of your life. People of many different traditions throughout history have found inner tranquility and equanimity—evenness despite outer conditions—through the practice of stillness; although their approaches have been different, the peace they sought is the same.

In this book, I will draw from these different traditions to help you build a stillness practice that you can easily incorporate into your busy life.

THE EVER-INCREASING NOISE

As technology advances, it simplifies parts of your life. But unfortunately, if we are not careful, it can also create more noise and stress. Electronic communications over multiple platforms can reach your phone at all hours of the day and night. Online retailers offer discounts in exchange for your email and phone number so they can advertise to you constantly. When you go for a walk in the park or in other places in nature where in the past you would not have been reachable, as long as your phone is in your pocket or bag, your social and professional responsibilities can follow you.

The noise of technology can also disturb your work. When notifications from social media or other applications continue to ping you throughout the day, your work can become very distracted and scattered. Sleep is often affected by all this noise; many people pick up their electronics late at night when they have difficulty sleeping. You may even find yourself staring at your phone when you would rather be connecting with your loved ones.

Some people have difficulty breaking away from social media, Netflix, video games, or other media. Indeed, many developers and content creators understand human psychology and behavior reinforcement very well.

As you can see, if you are not intentional about incorporating more stillness into your life, the noise of technology can take away your inner peace and distract you from what you value most.

The Benefits of a Stillness Practice

The regular practice of stillness can help you create peace inside even with all the noise and pressures that surround us today. As I mentioned, stillness practices have been serving humanity for many thousands of years, but in the past several decades there's been a worldwide explosion of interest in stillness practices. Physical, mental, and emotional wellness professionals have found stillness practices to be a powerful intervention in a broad range of situations, from general well-being to significant and chronic mental health diagnoses and other medical conditions. Research literature also touts the benefits of mindfulness-based interventions (therapeutic approaches that are grounded in mindfulness), compassion practices, and yoga in many different environments, including education, work, and clinical contexts.

In this section, I will discuss how a stillness practice can benefit your general well-being and physical health and help relieve stress, anxiety, and depression.

Well-Being

Stillness practices have been shown to help with well-being and social adjustment by increasing your ability to regulate your emotions; decreasing rumination (repetitive thoughts), which has been shown to improve psychological functioning; and helping release unhealthy habits and develop stronger, healthier habits. Practicing mindfulness, yoga, and self-compassion helps you show up for all your emotions in a kind, warm, and non-judgmental manner, which helps you identify, regulate, and accept emotions without being consumed by them. These stillness practices also help decrease self-criticism, internal reactivity, and internal conflict, which makes it easier to work toward your goals and get along better with others.

Physical Health

Stillness practices have been shown to improve physical health in a number of ways. Yoga, mindfulness practices, and prayer can increase heart rate variability and vagal tone (your ability to relax after stress), which are indicators of health and fitness. Mindfulness-based interventions have been shown to be effective in managing pain, overeating and binge eating, and tobacco and other substance use disorders. Self-management of chronic diseases such as hypertension, type 2 diabetes, and COPD has also been improved by mindfulness-based interventions. Yoga has been shown to benefit the relief of pregnancy-related discomfort, back pain, asthma, and cancer, as well as stroke rehabilitation.

Stress

Stillness practices can help you better deal with the many different stresses—family, academic, work, health, financial—we all encounter throughout our lives. Mindfulness, yoga, and compassion practices help build strength, equanimity, wisdom, and a feeling of interconnectedness that can carry you through the many storms of your life. Studies have shown that stillness practices help children, students, employees, health care workers, and patients better deal with the stresses they face in their lives. In fact, the first-ever mindfulness-based intervention was an eight-week program called mindfulness-based stress reduction (MBSR), which was created in the 1970s by Jon Kabat-Zinn and has been shown to help in a variety of contexts in which stress is an issue.

Anxiety

Mindfulness-based stress reduction, mindfulness-based cognitive therapy, compassion practices, and yoga have all shown benefits in treating anxiety disorders. One way these stillness practices reduce anxiety is by bringing you into the present moment and helping you release anxious thoughts about yourself, others, the world, and the future. Through regular mindfulness and compassion practices, people learn to create space for their anxious thoughts and sensations, which ultimately leads them to be less reactive with themselves and others. Imaging studies of mindfulness-based interventions in people with anxiety disorders demonstrate increased connectivity between brain structures that support more peace and less anxiety.

Depression

Mindfulness-based cognitive therapy has been shown to effectively treat major depressive disorder and decrease the risk of relapse at 60 weeks. In tandem, stillness and mindfulness-based interventions in general have been found to be superior to other active therapies and equivalent to other evidenced-based treatments, including cognitive behavior therapy and antidepressant medication. Yoga has also been found to be an effective treatment for depression. Depression is associated with high levels of connectivity in a higher-order brain network called the default mode network that is very involved in self-related processes like self-monitoring and self-judgement. Interestingly, default mode network activity and connectivity are reduced among experienced mindfulness meditators.

Key Takeaways

- Stillness has been practiced for many centuries in many different traditions and belief systems.

- Many of the Buddha's teachings are rooted in stillness practices. Mindfulness, or non-judgmental present-moment awareness, is an ancient Buddhist principle that is being taught and practiced in a variety of secular environments.

- Yoga is not just a physical practice; it also includes other components, including breathwork and meditation.

- Stoic philosophers beginning in ancient Greece understood the importance of equanimity, present-moment awareness, living a virtuous life, and self-reflection.

- Christian mystics have been practicing stillness since the beginning of the first millennium CE.

- Stillness practices teach you to live in the present moment by being grounded in your body and breath and showing up for yourself and others with warm and loving attention.

- Living in accordance with your values is an important part of creating inner stillness.

- Mindfulness, compassion practice, yoga, and prayer help many people live happier and healthier lives.

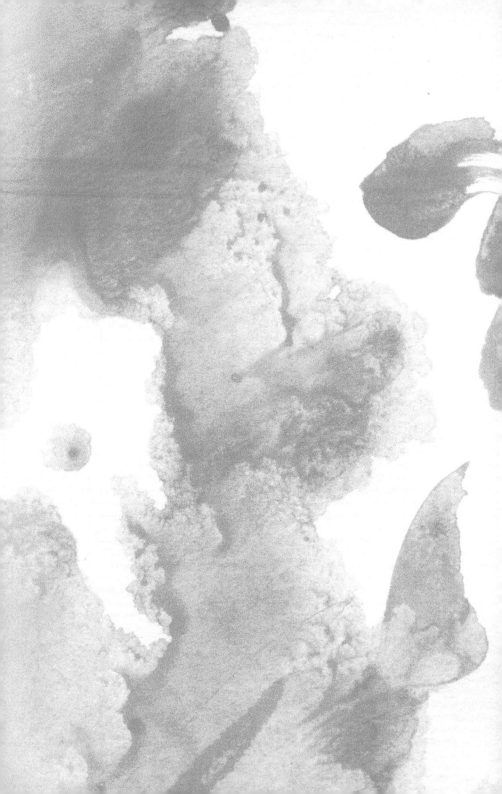

CHAPTER 2

Building a Stillness Practice

Now that you have a better understanding of the meaning, history, and benefits of stillness, you're ready for some guidance on how to best incorporate the practice of stillness into your life. The foundations you learn here will serve you well as you embark on the stillness practices in part 2 of this book. I will begin by discussing how you cultivate the first six principles of mindfulness: non-judging, letting go, non-striving, patience, trust, and acceptance. I'll then move on to the foundations of creating a regular practice, including making time, setting an intention, beginning again when you get distracted, and building endurance. I will discuss common challenges and obstacles to creating more peace and stillness in your life, including false expectations and perfectionism. I'll then share how this practice may unfold for you as you continue along your journey.

The Aspects of Stillness

Stillness is both a practice and a state of being; it unfolds differently for everyone. The seven principles of mindfulness are a great place to start. They can guide you, support you, and help you develop more inner stillness. These principles are all interdependent; cultivating one will support the cultivation of the others, and you can begin wherever you are. Building awareness around these principles and bringing mindfulness to your experience when you find that you are either in or out of alignment with these principles will help you on your path to creating more stillness in your life.

Here, I will discuss the first six principles of mindfulness, and I'll wrap up this chapter with a longer section on a discussion of the final principle of mindfulness—the Zen Buddhist principle of beginner's mind—so that this principle will be fresh in your mind as you embark on the stillness practices in part 2 of this book. Some of the stillness practices will dive deeper into these principles as well.

Non-Judging

Judgment is deeply ingrained in many of us. We have been conditioned to judge ourselves, others, and so much of what happens in our lives, often very harshly. Judgment is a very common way in which you fight or resist yourself, others, and the world, and this resistance leads to much of your suffering.

As you shine the light of awareness on your judgments of yourself and others and notice the sensations and emotions that surround them, they begin to dissolve. Rather than judging yourself for being judgmental, I recommend that you cultivate a kind and gentle awareness of the judgments you notice inside yourself as you do the stillness practices in part 2 of this book.

Letting Go

We all have ideas about what should have happened in the past, what will make us happy, how we and others should behave, what the world should look like, and how our lives should unfold. You can become so attached to these beliefs and desires that you neglect the beauty, richness, and power of the present moment. Many of us have difficulty letting go of attachments, and this clinging creates inner discontent. As you let go of these attachments, you release the resistance and discontent that you have created in your mind and find a peace and stillness deep within.

Non-Striving

Many of us have been conditioned from a young age to be constantly going, doing, and consuming. You may tie up your self-worth in your accomplishments, or you may have difficulty slowing down because the busyness is a distraction from difficult emotions that you would rather not experience. Some of us may have been taught that resting is lazy or weak. Despite all of your conditioning, we are human *beings*, not human *doings*, and part of healing is slowing down so you can hear the truth of your heart and soul. You are wise to balance your desire for growth and forward motion with deep self-love and acceptance.

Patience

Many of us struggle to force our lives in one direction or another. Just as you would damage a flower bud if you pried it open before it was ready, you may harm yourself or others when you try to force events to unfold on your timeline or in a way that you feel is best. We can become so focused on and consumed by our expectations and ideals that we put harmful pressure on ourselves and others. When you build awareness of your expectations and the pressure you place on yourself and others, you will become better able to release this forcing and live more patiently, in harmony with the truth of the present moment.

Trust

Many of us live with a lot of fear. We may worry a lot about ourselves, our relationships, our loved ones, our future, our health, work, school, the environment, politics, and/or current events. We may not trust that we will be able to handle all the challenges we encounter or that we will be okay in the context of these challenges. These fears and worries erode our trust in ourselves, others, and the world and create a lot of inner discontent and turmoil. You can learn to set down your fears and worries and choose to live more rooted in love and with a deep trust that you will be okay.

Acceptance

Acceptance is another difficult practice for so many of us, and it ties into many of the other principles that we have already discussed. Instead of accepting yourself, other people, and the world around you, you may find that you are wishing, pushing, trying to force situations and people—including yourself—to be different. And that is a losing battle. This isn't to say that you cannot work toward growth or progress in yourself and in the world, but rather that you are wise to balance growth and progress with love and acceptance. Many of us lean too far toward growth and progress (I'll accept this only when …), and this imbalance becomes resistance that keeps us in conflict with ourselves, others, and the world. The practice of acceptance helps you build peace and stillness inside your heart.

Building a Practice

If you want to cultivate stillness in your life, it takes effort. You will need to set a powerful intention, carve out time, begin again when you become distracted, and build endurance. If you have been fortunate enough to have some teaching or examples of stillness in your life, you may be a little farther along on the journey, but this book will still help you deepen or recommit to your practice.

Regrettably, much of our modern life does not support stillness practices. Society is constantly telling you what to purchase, consume, accomplish, or become, and the people around you may not understand the point of practicing stillness. They may see it as "doing nothing," even though you are doing something quite profound. In other words, there may be a lot of obstacles to developing a strong stillness practice. But, as we have seen, the rewards you reap will be well worth the time and effort.

Make Time

Choose a particular time when it will be easiest to commit to 15 minutes of daily stillness practice. Ideally, this should be a time when you are less likely to be disturbed and when you can plan to shut off all electronics. Perhaps you set your morning alarm 15 minutes earlier than you typically do or you schedule 15 minutes at lunchtime, right after you get home from work, or before bed. As with all habits, the first couple of weeks may require the most effort, but after the habit is formed, your stillness practice will become as automatic as brushing your teeth.

Set an Intention

Create a strong intention to incorporate a stillness practice into your life, and recall your intention throughout the day. You may wish to write down your intention and look at it every morning or place it somewhere where you will see it regularly. Commit to carving out 15 minutes every day for your formal practice of stillness, as well as incorporating the informal practice of stillness throughout your day—perhaps grounding yourself in the present moment and recalling the principles of stillness. Set your intention to create a strong stillness practice, and then be open to how it grows and unfolds over time.

Begin Again

Just as your heart beats, your mind produces thoughts. There is no way around this, and it doesn't mean that you are not good at meditation or that you are doing it wrong. While doing the stillness practices, you will find that your mind drifts away from the focus of the practice. When you notice this happening, whether it has been for 15 minutes or just one moment, bring a kind, gentle awareness to the departure and simply return to the practice. This principle of beginning again brings about much of the healing power of stillness practices.

Build Endurance

Understand that the process of creating a strong stillness practice is more of a marathon than a sprint. If you are unable to practice one day, let it go and begin again the next day. Celebrate all your successes, and release any tendency to be hard on yourself or beat yourself up. If you notice you are judging your stillness practice, recall the principle of non-judging and return to your intention. If you wake up late and only have two minutes, do two minutes. Arthur Ashe said it best: "Start where you are. Use what you have. Do what you can."

BE PRESENT

You spend so much of your time lost in thoughts of the past and planning or worrying about the future. But the past and the future are just concepts in your mind; the only moment you ever have is the present moment. When you spend so much time in your mind thinking about the past or future or how you wish this moment was different than it is, you create a lot of inner discontent. When you ground yourself in the present moment, you quiet your mind and become better able to show up for yourself, others, and the world with more love and attention.

What to Expect

Many people tell me that they tried meditation but couldn't do it or were not good at it because they were unable to clear their mind. As I mentioned, you can't stop your mind from creating thoughts any more than you can stop the ocean from creating waves. Your aim with stillness practice is to change your relationship with your thoughts rather than trying to stop them.

If we continue the ocean analogy, your aim is to become a better surfer. Some thoughts are horrible waves to surf, and you are wise to let these pass and ground yourself in the present moment and all the beauty that surrounds you. Other waves propel you forward toward your life goals and are awesome waves to ride—even while you stay very present on your surfboard. A stillness practice will enable you to see what is really going on—that the waves are not you—and will help you better choose which waves to surf and which to let pass.

You may bring your high expectations, timelines, and perfectionism to your stillness journey, but these don't serve you well here (or really, anywhere). Being a beginner can be very challenging. You may want to practice with perfect consistency and hope to see huge results right away. You may hope to do a seated practice for extended lengths of time from the get-go, then become frustrated when you feel too restless to continue. If you instead approach this gently, starting with five minutes and building up slowly, you set yourself up for success. Even if this sounds cheesy or corny, be a cheerleader for yourself, building yourself up and celebrating your small successes. Practice patience and trust, witnessing how your stillness practice blossoms and unfolds on its own timeline.

If you have a history of trauma and/or are finding stillness practice to be particularly stressful or aggravating, I recommend that you find a spiritually informed therapist you can work with.

HOW WILL I KNOW
IT'S WORKING?

Our typical ways of being in this world are deeply rooted in neural pathways that have fired in that pattern for generations and generations. These patterns manifest in deep ways from an early age. I say this not to discourage you but to encourage you to be gentle, kind, and patient with yourself as you set out on your journey to rewire the conditioning of generations.

Building more stillness in your life can be like charting a new path up a mountain. This new path doesn't have a clear direction, and there is a lot of foliage that you have to slowly clear away as you go. When you are tired, hungry, or stressed, you mindlessly veer back to the old path because you know it well and it is more comfortable to walk on. But when you are well-rested and clear, you can put in the effort to travel this new way of being—and the more time you spend on this path, the easier it becomes. Eventually, this new path is the more comfortable one. And the view on this new path is so breathtaking and amazing that you can't believe you ever took the old way.

The more present you become, the more peace you will feel in your heart. At first, you may notice that difficult moods are not as intense and don't last as long, and that you have more perspective when navigating challenges in your life. Your stillness will allow you to accomplish more and to live more in alignment with your values. You will notice that your attention and concentration begin to slowly improve, and that you begin to show up for yourself, others, and your work with a more compassionate, engaged, and powerful presence.

Your Stillness Toolbox

The purpose of this book is to help you incorporate more stillness into your life. To do that, you'll need some basic tools: meditation, breathwork, and visualization. The practices in part 2 of this book will vary in form and time commitment, but they all include elements of these three main tools. I will provide a brief introduction of each and discuss what they mean and how they apply to your practice of stillness.

Meditation

There are many ways to meditate, but most involve focusing and sustaining your attention on an object of meditation. This can be the feeling of your breath in your body, other sensations, thoughts, emotions, a mantra, a prayer, or phrases of loving-kindness to yourself and others. Meditation can also focus on the feeling of movement, as in walking meditation, other mindful movement practices, yoga asana practice, and meditative journaling, where you may reflect on a challenging experience or a spiritual idea. In open-awareness meditations, you bring your attention to any object that comes into awareness.

Breathwork

Breathwork is the conscious control of your breath for a particular aim. We'll focus on breathwork that helps calm your nervous system as well as the breath practices of yoga and mindful movement (there is quite a bit of overlap between these two types of breathwork). You can use your breath to calm your nervous system by taking long, slow exhales. This type of breathing increases the tone of your parasympathetic nervous system, which is the "rest and digest" system that balances your sympathetic nervous system—the "fight, flight, or freeze" system.

Visualization

Visualization uses the power of your creativity and imagination to create more inner stillness and peace. In loving-kindness meditation, you picture yourself and others receiving the healing wishes you send, which deepens your feelings of compassion. In some therapeutic stillness exercises, you visualize your older and wiser self loving and caring for a younger version of yourself at a difficult time in your life. In other stillness practices, you may visualize yourself forgiving another person or pursuing your goals or healing in your life.

Keeping a Beginner's Mind

Beginner's mind is one of the seven principles of mindfulness. This particular principle comes from the Chan and Zen Buddhist tradition. Beginner's mind teaches you to approach life much as a small child would: with openness and awe and devoted attention.

After being on this planet for many years, we develop a tendency to rely on concepts rather than reality. We see a tree, and instead of really looking at and opening to the presence of this unique and beautiful living organism, we quickly label it a tree and move on. We operate on the assumption that we know what trees are—and therefore we do not need to devote any of our attention to being fully present with the living being in front of us.

We do this with so much in our lives. Maybe you have oatmeal for breakfast, and because you have eaten oatmeal many times before, you go on automatic pilot, completely absorbed in your phone or your thoughts, and miss the entire experience of nourishing your body. This repeated absence in your own life creates an illusion of separation and ill-being.

Beginner's mind teaches you to show up for all moments with an open mind—even the ones you assume are not conceptually interesting. When you show up in this way, you begin to live much more in the present moment and are less trapped in the concepts of your mind. You become more grounded in the actual present and are able to access a lot more wisdom and joy, whether you are eating, working, or spending time with your loved ones. You learn to see each moment in your fluid, changing reality for what it is, and you are less likely to stay stuck in static and unchanging concepts. Approaching life with beginner's mind is a powerful way to live.

Key Takeaways

- Non-judging, letting go, non-striving, patience, trust, and acceptance are principles that help you create more stillness and peace inside yourself.

- Making time, setting an intention, beginning again, and building endurance are important parts of building a strong stillness practice.

- The goal of stillness practice is less about clearing your mind and more about shifting your relationship to your thoughts.

- Letting go of perfectionism and celebrating even small successes will support you in developing a strong stillness practice.

- If you have a history of trauma or find this practice to be particularly stressful or aggravating, find a spiritually informed therapist to help guide you on this journey.

- Regularly practicing stillness will help you show up in your life in a more powerful and peaceful way.

- Meditation, breathwork, and visualization are the tools of stillness practice.

- Beginner's mind encourages you to be attentive and open-minded in your life.

PART TWO

50 Practices for Stillness

Welcome to part 2, where we will dive into 50 practices to create more stillness in your life. I recommend starting at the beginning and working your way to the end, because the earlier practices cover basic principles that later practices will build on. With that being said, feel free to jump to a particular practice if it calls out to you.

These practices will last anywhere from 5 to 15 minutes and will take many different forms, including several types of meditation, movement practices (such as yoga), journaling, spiritual study, and self-reflection. The times listed for each practice are general recommendations, so feel free to modify the time if you feel less or more is needed. Take time to read the instructions before beginning an exercise.

Spending time with these stillness practices is a beautiful way to invest in yourself. May your practice bring you more love and peace.

Let's get started!

Mindfulness of the Breath

Mindfulness of the breath is a beautiful stillness practice to begin with. You are always breathing, and you can bring your attention to your breath in any setting, whether you are alone in your room, in a meeting, or in a crowded public place. But the more time you carve out for formal practice, the easier it will become to be grounded in the present in informal settings and throughout your life.

1. Choose a time and a place where there will be relatively minimal disruptions and distractions. It doesn't have to be completely quiet or away from others, but any degree of quiet that you can create will support your practice.

2. Find a supportive chair in which you can sit comfortably, either cross-legged or with both feet flat on the floor. If you prefer to sit on the floor, perhaps a cushion or pillow under your bottom will feel more supportive.

3. You may wish to face a window or even create a special setting for your stillness practice. Perhaps design an altar where you can place items or images that are of spiritual significance to you.

4. Set five minutes on your watch, your phone, or a kitchen timer.

5. Sit upright in a relaxed posture.

6. Close your eyes if it feels comfortable. If you prefer to keep your eyes open, you may wish to lower your gaze and soften your focus.

7. Bring your attention to wherever you feel your breath most pleasantly in your body. Perhaps this is in your belly as it rises and falls. Or maybe you concentrate on the sides of your chest as it expands and then contracts. You may also focus on the top of your chest as it moves up and down or simply feel your breath as it enters and exits your nostrils.

8. Maintain your attention on the movement of your breath in your body. Don't try to control your breathing; just pay attention as your body breathes on its own.

9. When you notice that your mind has wandered to other places, simply note it and then kindly and gently bring your attention back to your breath. At times you may respond with some irritation or judgment when you have discovered that you are deep in thought and have lost track of your breath. See whether you can release any resistance and begin again.

10. When the timer sounds, take a couple of breaths before jumping up and moving on to the next item on your schedule.

Start Small: It's best to start with five minutes, since that makes it easier to stick to your commitment. Daily practice is the most powerful. Try to slowly increase the amount of time you sit. Sitting upright with a straight spine, preferably away from the back of the chair, fosters wakefulness.

Awareness of Sense Perceptions

10 minutes

Your senses are always in the here and now. As you practice awareness of what you can feel, smell, see, and hear, you focus on the present and build more peace. Many of us spend so much time lost in thoughts and preoccupied with their content. However, thoughts are fleeting, often illusory, and can cause a lot of suffering. When you dedicate time to ground yourself in the present moment, you empower yourself to live with more clarity.

1. Start this practice in a designated meditation area where you are relatively protected from disruptions and distractions.

2. Sit in an upright and comfortable posture.

3. Close your eyes if that feels comfortable, or lower your gaze and soften your focus.

4. Bring your attention to the places where your body makes contact with other surfaces. Can you feel where your feet meet the floor, chair, or cushion? What does this feel like? Can you describe the sensation?

5. Can you feel other places where your body contacts surfaces? Is your bottom or your back contacting a surface? How does this feel? Is it different from the sensations of contact that your feet have?

6. Where are your arms and hands resting? What are the sensations present there?

7. Can you feel your hands and fingers from the inside? Do you know they are there without looking at them?

8. If you notice any pain or discomfort, see whether you can stay present with the dynamic sensations. Can you describe the qualities of the pain? Do they change at all over time? Can you bring any loving compassion to the pain?

9. Bring your attention to whatever sounds may be present. Notice whether they are consistent or intermittent. Does the quality of the sounds change with time? Do you notice a positive, negative, or neutral reaction to these sounds?

10. Are there any smells around you? Can you describe them (rather than labeling them)? What are your reactions to these smells?

11. Open your eyes and look around. What objects do you see? What are the shapes and colors of these objects? What are your reactions to these sights? Bring your attention to the movement of your breath in your body for a couple of breaths.

12. Give yourself a moment to pause and settle into all your senses. Bring this peace with you as you move forward in your day.

Grounding for Anxiety: Focusing on your senses is a portable skill that you can use when you are feeling stressed, anxious, overwhelmed, or panicked in any setting. Feel your breath in your body and the places where your body makes contact with other surfaces. Note the sights, sounds, and smells around you.

Introduction to Mindful Movement

5 minutes

A formal stillness practice can be stationary or moving. Many meditation classes and retreats alternate sitting practice with walking practice. You can also practice staying present in a yoga asana practice and with many other types of movement. When you designate time for mindful movement, you practice creating peace in movement, which is carried into your daily activities. Practicing mindful movement before doing a seated meditation can also help quiet your mind in your meditation.

1. Read through the following instructions before beginning. You may also wish to look at photographs of these poses on my website, AMindfulMD.com.

2. This can be done standing or seated in a chair. Place your feet flat on the floor at the width of your hips.

3. Begin with your hands down at your sides in an easy standing/sitting pose. On your inhale, sweep your hands up above your head with your palms facing each other—the yoga mountain pose. If you cannot sweep your hands above your head, go as far as is comfortable. Breathe here.

4. Turn your pinky fingers in toward each other to expand the space between your shoulder blades.

5. On your exhale, float your arms back down to easy standing/sitting pose.

6. Inhale and raise your arms back above your head to mountain pose, and continue to move your arms with your breath for five inhales and exhales.

7. On your sixth inhale, return to mountain pose. On your exhale, press your palms together, move your hands down to the level of your heart (this is called heart center), bend at your hips, and then reach your arms toward the floor. This is forward fold pose. If you are standing, maintain a soft bend in your knees to release the tension from your lower back.

8. Seated or standing, pause here in forward fold. Feel any tension in your lower back and/or your hamstrings melt from your body. Hang your head heavy and feel the release in the muscles at the top of your neck. Move your head from side to side, bringing your left ear to your left arm and then your right ear to your right arm.

9. When you feel ready to move on, slowly rise up to a straight spine, stacking one vertebra at a time on the top of the next.

10. When you come to sitting or standing upright, bring your hands again to heart center. This is standing/ sitting at attention pose, where you typically set an intention.

Setting an Intention: At the beginning of yoga asana practice, you typically pause to set an intention for the remainder of the practice. What is your intention for the rest of your day? Would you like to dedicate the rest of the day to a special person or a particular mindset?

Calm Breathing

There are certain breathing techniques that can bring you more calm and peace by activating the parasympathetic nervous system. Many people live with a hyperactive sympathetic nervous system—the system that activates your fight, flight, or freeze responses. The parasympathetic nervous system balances the sympathetic nervous system and can be activated by working on the intensity or length of your exhale. When you carve out time to breathe in this way, you bring more peace and stillness to your nervous system.

1. We'll start with a lion's breath, a yogic breathing technique. Take a deep inhale through your nose and then open your mouth wide, stick your tongue out and down toward your chin, and exhale forcefully, making a loud "ha" sound.

2. Breathe normally for a couple of breaths, and then repeat the lion's breath a few more times.

3. Return to normal breath for a few moments.

4. Take a slow, deep inhale for a count of four.

5. Pause at the end of the inhale for a count of four.

6. Exhale as slowly as you can through pursed lips.

7. Repeat that sequence—inhale for a count of four, hold for a count of four, and exhale as slowly as you can through pursed lips—for five breaths. Can you extend your exhale to six or eight seconds?

8. If you notice your mind wandering to other thoughts, gently and kindly return your focus to the breathing practice.

9. Now you will practice another yogic breathing technique called Ujjayi breathing, in which you breathe with a constriction at the back of your throat. You create this same constriction when you use your breath to fog up a window; now try doing the constriction with your mouth closed, breathing through your nose. You may notice an oceanic sound with this breath.

10. Practice Ujjayi breathing for five breaths with long, slow exhales. You may notice it is easier to do this constriction on exhales, which is fine.

11. Try the breath sequence in step 7 with a shorter hold at the top of the inhale, perhaps for two seconds instead of four. You can also try this breath sequence with another hold of two or four seconds at the bottom of the exhale.

12. Finish the practice with box breathing: Inhale for a count of four, hold at the top of the inhale for a count of four, exhale for a count of four, and hold at the bottom of the exhale for a count of four.

13. Continue to practice these different breathing techniques, and reflect on which was most calming or helpful for you.

Calming Yourself: Breathing practices that activate your parasympathetic nervous system bring calm to your body and can be particularly helpful when you are dealing with difficult emotions. If you are experiencing fear, anger, or sadness and find mindfulness practices difficult, you may wish to use these breathing techniques to calm and nurture yourself.

Body Scan

The body scan is an important part of a stillness practice. Practicing the body scan regularly has been shown to help with physical pain, stress, and sleep problems. You began practicing awareness of sense perceptions in the second practice (Awareness of Sense Perceptions, page 32), and you will use those same skills here in the body scan, where you will notice the sensations in your entire body, part by part. The body scan is different from many other stillness practices because it is often practiced lying on your back.

1. Try to practice at a time and place where you will not be disturbed.

2. In the body scan, you start at the top of your head and move slowly down your body, feeling into each part. Read through all the instructions first. Then put the book down and try it for yourself.

3. Set your timer for 15 minutes and lie on your back. Feel free to use pillows or blankets to find a comfortable position.

4. Gently close your eyes. Focus your attention on the top of your head, your forehead, and your temples, and notice any sensations. Can you feel any energy, any tightness or softness? Can you feel the temperature? Does this area feel more cold, neutral, or warm? If there is any discomfort or pain present, can you stay with the sensations? What is the quality of the discomfort/pain? Is it consistent over time, or does it change at all?

5. Move your attention to the rest of your face: your eyes, cheeks, ears, jaw, and mouth. What do you notice?

6. Move to your neck and your shoulders. What is present here?

7. Move your attention down first one arm and then the other. Notice what is present in the shoulder, upper arm, elbow, forearm, wrist, hand, palm, and the length of the fingers.

8. Bring your attention to your chest. What sensations are present? Then your upper back. What do you notice here?

9. Move to your belly. What do you notice here? Then your lower back. What sensations are present?

10. Move into your pelvic area and note what you feel. Then move your attention to your bottom. What do you notice here?

11. Now move down one leg and then the other. Start at the top of your leg and focus on the front and back of your thigh. Move to your knee and then the front and back of your calf. Then your ankle, then the top and bottom of each foot. Can you feel your toes?

Inhabiting Your Body: Try this practice daily for at least 15 minutes for two weeks. You may wish to do the body scan as you are trying to fall asleep, but please also make sure you are setting aside time for this practice when you are fully awake. As you practice more, does your experience change at all?

Walking Meditation

10 minutes

As you build up your stillness practice, you may wish to practice for longer periods on some days. On these days, alternating sitting practice with walking meditation can be powerful. In walking meditation, you become very present with the sensations in your body as you walk. The more you practice walking meditation, the more you will be able to bring mindfulness into your daily life when you move about in the course of your day. If walking is challenging for you, you may wish to concentrate on seated movement, such as in Introduction to Mindful Movement (page 34). If you move around with a wheelchair or other support, you can practice moving mindfully with these supports.

1. Choose a stretch of no more than 20 feet where you can walk. I recommend you pick a place where there will be minimal disruptions and distractions. You can do this in your home or outside, preferably somewhere relatively private, if that's possible.

2. Set a timer for 10 minutes.

3. Begin your walking meditation by walking at a much slower pace than you would typically walk. If you feel comfortable doing so, maintain your gaze at a point down and in front of your walking path.

4. Ground yourself in the sensations of your body. Notice the movement of your body through space. What part of your foot first contacts the earth? How does the contact feel in your foot? What is the other foot doing when this happens?

5. Notice your foot as it lifts from the earth. Which part leaves the ground first? Second? How does your foot move through space? Where are you holding your weight? How does the foot on the ground feel when the other foot lifts?

6. Notice your foot as it comes back down again. Where is your other foot? What happens next?

7. When you reach the end of your walking path, simply turn your body around and walk back the way you came. Continue walking back and forth, focusing on the sensations and movements in your body as you move. Notice that when you pay attention in this way, each step is entirely new.

8. If you notice that your mind has wandered, note where it is, then gently and kindly return your attention to your walking meditation.

9. Try picking up your pace, and see whether you notice any different sensations or movements.

10. As your feet move, what is the rest of your body doing? How do your hips move? What does the left hip do when the left foot lifts? What about when the right foot lifts? What are the sensations in your knees, thighs, belly, etc.?

Deepening Your Practice: A lot of people love doing walking meditation in beautiful outdoor settings. Can you feel the wind, rain, or sunshine on your skin? What are your emotional reactions to what is present? If you notice any pain with walking, does the pain shift or change at all over time?

Loving-Kindness Meditation

15 minutes

There is a saying that if mindfulness is one wing of the bird, then loving-kindness meditation is the other wing. In loving-kindness meditation, you offer up good wishes for yourself, loved ones, neutral people, difficult people, and people all over the world. Loving-kindness meditation can be powerful medicine for fear and anger, and it is a beautiful practice to do when you are out in public places, silently offering these phrases to people you see.

1. Write the following phrases (or any version that resonates deeply with you) on a sheet of paper for reference:

    May I/you be safe and protected, free from internal harm and external threat.

    May I/you be physically healthy, vital, and full of life.

    May I/you be truly happy and deeply peaceful.

    May I/you live my/your life with ease.

2. Find your designated meditation area and read through all the instructions before starting.

3. Set your timer for 15 minutes.

4. Sit in a comfortable posture. Close your eyes if you feel comfortable doing so, or lower your gaze and soften your focus.

5. Start your practice with loving-kindness meditation for yourself. Picture yourself in your mind's eye. Offer the phrases in step 1 slowly, one by one, to yourself. As you do so, imagine smiling at yourself and soaking up the radiance you see in yourself.

6. Move then to a loved one. Pick someone for whom it is easy to have loving feelings. Children, dear friends, mentors, and spiritual figures make for great loved ones. Picture this person gazing lovingly at you. Offer the phrases for your loved one. Imagine this person receiving all this love and kindness from you and beaming a large smile back at you.

7. Pick a neutral person, someone you don't have strong feelings for one way or the other. Baristas, store clerks, and people you see on your commute tend to be good neutral people. Repeat the phrases for your neutral person. Imagine them receiving these wishes.

8. Choose a difficult person, but not the most difficult person. Maybe a 6 on a scale of 1 to 10. Offer the phrases for this person and imagine them receiving them with a smile.

9. Now imagine that you, your loved one, your neutral person, and your difficult person are all standing together in a circle. Offer the phrases to all people everywhere.

Warming Your Heart: Loving-kindness meditation can transform your heart from the inside out. If you repeat this practice daily for two weeks and choose the same neutral person, what do you notice about your feelings toward the neutral person at the end of the two weeks? What do you notice if you do the same with a difficult person?

Awareness of Thoughts

10 minutes

We have been conditioned to give our thoughts a lot of power; many of us feel very defined by our thoughts, believing that they are very personal and a reflection of who we truly are. One of my favorite proverbs is "The mind is a wonderful servant but a poor master." Thoughts are fleeting, are often untrue, and can be harmful. Many of our thoughts come from how we were raised, our culture, and the media. Here you use your thoughts as the focus of your meditation.

1. Find your designated meditation area. Sit comfortably.

2. Set your timer for 10 minutes.

3. Close your eyes if that feels comfortable, or lower your gaze and soften your focus.

4. Take a couple of slow, deep breaths with a long exhale.

5. Return your breathing to its normal rhythm.

6. Bring your attention to the movement of your breath in your body for a few breaths.

7. Now shift your attention to your thoughts. When you first bring your attention to your thoughts, there may not be a lot of thoughts present. "There's not a lot of thoughts present" is a thought.

8. When a thought arises, bring your attention to it. See whether you can notice any judgment or evaluation of the thought that arises. "I like this thought." "This is a bad thought." These are more thoughts.

9. Try to let go of the judgments and evaluations and simply notice the thoughts, perhaps as if they are leaves floating down a river or clouds moving through the sky.

10. "I am not good at this meditation" is another thought.

11. Notice any emotions that arise with certain thoughts.

12. If you find that you get lost in thought, bring awareness to this. Notice how some thoughts seem to be a lot more stickier than other thoughts. If you believe it would be helpful, return your attention to your breath for a couple of breaths, and then, when you feel ready, return to noticing your thoughts.

13. If any traumatic or very triggering thoughts arise, you can open your eyes if that feels safer. You may wish to do some of the breathing techniques from Calm Breathing (page 36) or grounding practices from Awareness of Sense Perceptions (page 32).

14. If you find this or other meditation practices to be too triggering, feel free to skip them. I also recommend that you find a spiritual teacher or a psychotherapist to further explore these triggers.

THINK: The acronym THINK is a helpful rubric as you bring more awareness to your thoughts. As you notice your thoughts, you can ask: Is this thought True? Is it Helpful? Is it Inspiring? Is it Necessary? Is it Kind?

Releasing Tension in the Head and Neck

5 minutes

So many of us hold stress in the muscles of the head and neck. You may clench your jaw, grind your teeth, or perhaps carry tension in your neck. As you pay more attention to your body, your awareness of this tension will grow, and with intention and practice you can begin to slowly release this tension. As you shed this unnecessary constriction from your being, you will begin to travel lighter.

1. Find a quiet space with few to no distractions. You can sit in a chair or on the floor, possibly on a cushion for more comfort.

2. Open and close your mouth a couple of times, noticing any tension in the muscles of your jaw around your temples. As you notice the tension and open your mouth, set the intention to release this tension. Lightly close your mouth and your eyes and inhale. Imagine drawing the rich, oxygenated, healing breath to any tension present in the jaw muscles around your temples. On your exhale, release this tension.

3. Smile widely with an open mouth, the corners of your mouth reaching as far toward your ears as possible. Relax and repeat a couple of times. Notice any tension present in your jaw muscles right in front of your ears or in the muscles of your face around your eyes, mouth, and forehead. Make any intuitive movements of the muscles of your jaw and your face (for example, scrunch up your forehead, open your eyes wide, squeeze your eyes shut, make a kissy face) with the intention to notice

and release any tension that's present. Close your eyes, relax your muscles, and inhale into the areas of tension. On your exhale, release that tension.

4. Drop your left ear to your left shoulder, then slowly roll your head forward to your chest, then to the right, bringing your right ear to your right shoulder. Continue the roll with the back of your head moving toward your back, and then your left ear ultimately moving back to your left shoulder. If this is comfortable, repeat a couple of times in this direction and then a couple of times in the reverse direction. Inhale as you roll your head forward, exhale as you roll backward.

5. If you find any tension, lengthen the muscle where the tension is present. Imagine drawing your inhale to this area, and on your exhale release that tension.

Warm Water Tension Release: Try this exercise in a warm bath or shower. If you are in the bath, you may wish to try some aromatherapy bath salts; in the shower, maybe a soothing body wash. Linger in the areas where you feel tension. Give your muscles time and breath to lengthen and relax.

Journaling

15 minutes

Journaling is an important tool for stillness. If you are lost in anxious thoughts, journaling can help you slow down by stopping to put your thoughts down on paper, addressing what you can, and releasing the rest. Writing can also help you pursue your truth and express, explore, and process any powerful feelings deep inside yourself. Writing can also be creative and can help you pursue your goals and gain greater perspective and clarity in your life.

1. Find a place where you can write/read/reflect relatively uninterrupted, either on paper or on a computer.

2. Set a timer for 15 minutes.

3. Pick an issue or concern from your life that has been troubling you or that often comes up in your thoughts.

4. Write down whatever comes to mind, trying not to censor yourself.

5. After you have been writing for about five to seven minutes, wrap up your thoughts and then read through everything you have written.

6. If, after reading what you have written, you want to add anything more, do so.

7. Pause for a moment. Read it all again if you would like to.

8. Consider the following questions, and if any of them strike you as particularly relevant, continue writing in response to them.

9. Did your writing offer you any greater clarity on the situation?

10. Did any emotions come up while you were writing? Were any of the emotions surprising? Were you able to express any of these emotions? Do you believe there are more emotions present that need to be processed or expressed? If so, can you schedule more time to write on these feelings or speak to a trusted friend, family member, spiritual teacher, or psychotherapist?

11. What are the aspects of the situation that you do not have control over? Are you able to release any worries or aspects of the situation that you don't have control over? If you don't have control over some parts of the situation, are they worth your peace? Is there any other way to think about these factors? Using the THINK acronym from Awareness of Thoughts (page 44), are your thoughts about this situation true, helpful, inspiring, necessary, and kind? Can you release the thoughts that are not serving you?

12. What aspects of the situation do you have control over?

13. Do you have any ideas on how to move forward?

14. Have your feelings about this situation changed at all?

15. Is there anything you would like to write more about?

Find Your Wisdom: The wisdom deep inside you is profound. When you call on your higher self—your intuition, your inner wisdom—to help you address the difficulties in your life, you begin to build trust in your ability to deal with all that you face in life. Journaling is a powerful way to access this wisdom.

The Seven Principles of Mindfulness

15 minutes

The seven principles of mindfulness are acceptance, trust, patience, letting go, beginner's mind, non-striving, and non-judging. These qualities help create more peace, love, and joy in your heart, mind, and soul. Unfortunately, many of us have been conditioned to value qualities that are in direct opposition to the principles of mindfulness, such as striving, judging, and fixing. In this stillness practice, you can begin to investigate and nurture these principles of mindfulness in yourself.

1. Find a quiet place where you will be able to write either on paper or on a computer.

2. Write down each of the principles and what it means to you. For example, for acceptance you may write about releasing resistance. Then consider the following questions for each principle and write freely. (If you would like more direction, you may refer back to the section on the seven principles of mindfulness in chapter 2.)

3. Were you taught this principle when you were growing up by your caregivers, your family, or your friends? Does your culture emphasize the importance of this principle? Do you see this principle reflected in the media? Is there anyone in your life who encourages this principle in you now? Do you encourage this principle in others?

4. How strong do you believe you are when it comes to this principle?

5. Who in your life manifests this principle in a strong way? (You don't need to know these people personally,

and they can be living or passed. Feel free to choose historical figures, celebrities, or spiritual teachers.) How do these individuals model this principle in their life?

6. Is this principle important to you?

7. Is this principle important to humankind? Would humanity benefit from having more of this principle? How so?

8. Are there any ways you could become stronger in this principle? How could you nurture this principle in your life? Is there anything you could regularly incorporate into your life that would help you build your practice of this principle? Are there any daily practices that could help? What small and achievable goals could you set to help support you?

9. Do you want to teach any children or young people in your life this principle?

10. Now, considering all seven mindfulness principles, which principle comes most easily for you? Which is the most difficult? Which principle feels the most important to strengthen now? Can you commit to one stillness practice that you can practice daily to strengthen this principle? What do you plan to do? Write down your thoughts on a sticky note, and place it somewhere you see regularly.

Positive Change: Visualize yourself embracing the seven principles of mindfulness. How does this manifest in your thoughts, emotions, behaviors, and relationship to yourself and others? How does embracing these principles create positive change in your emotional health? What other benefits in your life do you see when you embrace these principles?

Eating in Stillness

5 minutes

Many of us eat most of our meals with a host of distractions. Perhaps you eat while reading, watching TV, looking online, working, or commuting. Listening to the inner wisdom of your body can be very difficult with all these distractions. Your entire relationship with food can be improved dramatically by starting to bring mindfulness to eating. Here we start with the basics of mindful eating, and in future practices we'll build on these same principles.

1. This practice is typically done with a raisin. If you don't have a raisin, choose a similar food, such as a grape, a berry, or a small piece of a different fruit, dried or fresh.

2. Find a quiet place with minimal to no distractions.

3. Place the piece of fruit in your hand. Use your visual sense to look closely at it. What do you notice? How does it look? Describe the color, shape, and any other qualities it has.

4. What does the fruit feel like in your hand? Is it smooth or rough? How would you describe the texture?

5. Consider the path it took to get to you. Where did it grow? Who may have tended to the plants on which it grew? How was it harvested? How did it get from where it grew to your hand? Who was involved? Did you buy the fruit, and if so, where and from whom? How many people were involved in providing you with this small piece of fruit?

6. Hold the fruit up to your nose. What does it smell like? Do you notice any internal sensations as you smell the fruit?

7. Without chewing, place the piece of fruit in your mouth. What does it feel like on your tongue? What do you notice is happening in your mouth? What impulses do you notice?

8. Start to slowly chew the piece of fruit without completely chewing it up and swallowing. What do you notice? Can you describe the taste? Is it difficult to eat slowly like this? As you chew, how does the fruit change? What are the textures?

9. Finish chewing and slowly swallow. What movements do you notice in your mouth? What muscular actions are happening?

10. After swallowing, pause for a moment. If you have more fruit, do you want more? Do you feel hungry? What do you notice in your body?

Listen to Your Body: Try to continue your mindful eating practice. Choose at least one snack or meal a day where you eliminate distractions and dedicate your full attention to the process of eating. Listen to the cues of your body, and eat slowly and intentionally. Stay present with all the different sensations.

Releasing Tension in the Body

10 minutes

You practiced releasing tension from your head and neck on page 46, and now we bring this practice to your shoulders, lower back, and hamstrings, which can store stress and trauma from your past. When you regularly check in with your body, maintain correct alignment, and stretch and lengthen your muscles, you access deep healing that encompasses the whole of your being.

1. Read through these instructions before beginning. You may also wish to look at photographs of these poses on my website, AMindfulMD.com.

2. Start by standing with your arms by your side and your palms facing forward. You can also do this sitting in a chair.

3. Pull your shoulders up by your ears, pause for a moment, and notice how this feels. When you are stressed, your shoulders may creep up toward your ears.

4. Now relax your shoulders back and down, and broaden the space across your chest by rolling your shoulders back slightly. Take a couple of breaths here, and check in with how this feels.

5. Move between these two positions a couple of times, noticing any differences.

6. Now sit on the floor with your legs stretched out straight in front of you, or remain in your chair. Inhale and lift your hands above your head lengthen your spine toward the ceiling, and on your exhale, bend forward at your hips over your legs. Start with a bend in your knees to stretch your lower back. Take a few breaths.

7. On your next inhale, lengthen your spine forward (so you are still bent but your spine is straight, with as much distance from your hips to your shoulders as possible), and on the exhale, hinge forward at your hips, bringing your torso closer to your thighs. Continue lengthening your spine on your inhale and folding forward on your exhale for a couple of breaths.

8. If it feels comfortable in your lower back, begin to straighten your knees as much as is comfortable to stretch more through the backs of your thighs (the hamstrings). Hold this pose for several breaths.

9. Gently release and lie on your back. Pull your knees in to your belly. Stretch your arms out to either side with your palms facing down, gently drop your knees over to the left, and, if it's comfortable, turn your head to gaze over your right shoulder. This is an easy supine twist. Breathe into the opening across your lower back for a couple of breaths.

10. Come back to center, then drop your knees to the right and gaze over your left shoulder. Breathe here.

11. If you are in a chair, place your left hand on your left hip and your right hand on the outside of your left knee, and gently twist to the left, gazing over your left shoulder if that feels comfortable. Repeat on the other side.

12. Come back to center, and wait a few moments before you get up.

Relaxing into Alignment: As you move through your day, notice the position of your shoulders. Particularly when you are feeling stressed, your shoulders may start to creep up toward your ears. If you find your shoulders close to your ears, roll them back and down, and broaden the space across your chest.

Mindful Morning Routine

15 minutes

If you can start your mornings with stillness and set beautiful, strong intentions for your day, your life will be transformed. I recommend waking up a little while before you need to start getting yourself and others ready for the day so you can dedicate some time to nourishing your emotional, physical, and spiritual health before you do anything else. Carving out even 15 minutes before your day officially begins can make a world of difference.

1. Your goal is to get to your chair or meditation cushion as soon as possible after waking up. If you need to first use the bathroom, get some water, take medication, or attend to any other necessary self-care tasks, do so. However, before you do anything more, head straight for your stillness practice area.

2. Choose a seated meditation from any stillness practice. This could be Mindfulness of the Breath (page 30), Awareness of Sense Perceptions (page 32), a brief Loving-Kindness Meditation (page 42), or Awareness of Thoughts (page 44). Feel free to flip back in the book to the stillness practice you choose for reference before you begin. Set your timer for five minutes.

3. Spend five minutes in seated stillness practice.

4. When the timer goes off, open your eyes if they were closed, and pause for a couple of moments. Look around you and soak in the quiet. If you are near a window, perhaps gaze outside and appreciate what you can see.

5. After a couple of moments, set your timer for five minutes and spend this time in some form of moving stillness practice. If you wish, you can do Walking Meditation (page 40), and if weather and other conditions permit, you may even wish to go outside for this time. Being outside in the morning can be powerful medicine. If you prefer to do some moving mountain poses from Introduction to Mindful Movement (page 34), inhale as you bring your arms up to mountain pose, then exhale as you float your arms down by your sides. You can also stretch into the muscles of your face, head, neck, shoulders, back, or hamstrings to release any tension.

6. When your five minutes of mindful movement are over, find your journal, or simply say aloud or silently to yourself what intention you would like to bring with you into your day. Consider whether you wish for more peace, love, connection, clarity, calm, joy, creativity, or passion, or whether you would like to dedicate your day to a loved one. Spend several minutes considering this intention, either by writing or by speaking.

A Powerful Way to Start Your Day: Starting out, you may be able to dedicate only 15 minutes to stillness practices in the mornings. As you continue your practice, you may wish to slowly increase the time you spend in both seated and moving stillness practices. This small investment will reap huge rewards.

Awareness of Emotions

Emotions are powerful and underlie so many of the decisions that we make in our lives. But many people struggle to name, understand, and express their emotions. As you build more awareness of your emotions, you empower yourself to be clearer and more effective in your life.

1. Read through all the following instructions before beginning.

2. Find your seated stillness space, and set a timer for 10 minutes.

3. Close your eyes if that feels comfortable, or lower your gaze and soften your focus.

4. Take a few deep breaths with long, slow exhales.

5. Return to your normal breathing rhythm, and practice Mindfulness of the Breath (page 30) for a few breaths.

6. Bring your awareness to any emotions that may be present. Do you notice any fear, calm, anger, love, excitement, sadness, joy, disgust, grief, or variations on these?

7. If you notice more than one emotion, choose the strongest one. Stay with and observe the emotion as much as possible.

8. If you notice any thoughts (any description longer than one word is likely a thought; emotions are usually one word), try to let them go and return to the emotion.

9. Where do you notice the emotion in your body? Is it in your head, throat, chest, belly? What does it feel like? If you could give it a color, what color would it be? Is the emotion constant, or does it change with time? Is there a temperature associated with it?

10. If thoughts keep coming up, note the emotional tone of the thoughts. Emotions often drive thoughts of a similar emotional tone.

11. Notice any internal reactions to the emotion. Is there any judgment, resistance, or aversion? Do you believe you shouldn't have the feeling? Do you wish it would go away? Or do you believe that perhaps something is wrong with you for having the emotion? If you notice any of these reactions, simply take note, let go, and come back to the direct experience of the emotion in your body.

12. This may be more subtle and difficult to observe, but do you notice any clinging to the emotion, particularly if it's an emotion you enjoy?

13. Keep releasing any thoughts and staying with the emotions. Over the course of your meditation, have your emotions changed at all? How so?

Emotional Intelligence: Practicing awareness of emotions regularly will enhance your ability to name, understand, hold, process, and communicate your emotions. When you develop these emotional abilities, you harness the power of your emotions to create meaningful change in your health, relationships, and work.

Awareness of Ego

In spiritual practice, we speak of your ego as your little self. It's the part of you that feels small, incomplete, and insecure, and because of this, it fights against reality, wanting to accumulate more of what it expects will make it feel better and pushing away whatever it is afraid of. If you become acquainted with this part of yourself, you are better able to pause and find clarity, rather than letting your ego run the show.

1. Set yourself up in a quiet area with few to no distractions where you can write, either on paper or on a computer.

2. Use the following questions as writing prompts.

3. What do you notice about your ego? When is it loud? What does it want? What does it dislike?

4. Egos relish being right. Recall a situation in your life when you really wanted to be right or you relished being right. Your ego was probably very active in this situation. Write about how your ego was present in a situation in which you were very focused on being right.

5. Egos also like to fight reality and are really focused on hypothetical ideals. Do you remember any situations when you really wanted a certain thing to happen, perhaps a relationship, job, school program, or project? Do you recall any of these situations in which the thing you really wanted ended up not being good for you? Write about how your ego was present in this situation.

6. Egos always want more and cannot be satisfied. Write about how your ego may become active when it comes to consuming large amounts of food, alcohol, other substances, TV, video games, or sex. Does this leave you feeling content and peaceful?

7. Egos can also get really focused on what they perceive will be bad for them. What is something in your life that you fought, resisted, or dreaded but perhaps turned out just fine or maybe even positive? Write about how your ego played a part in this situation.

8. Do you ever find yourself comparing yourself to others, feeling either less than or superior to other people? Is this typically an activity that helps support your emotional and spiritual well-being? How might your ego be present here?

9. Egos feel very fearful, because they believe they are separate from the rest of life. Are there situations where you find it very difficult to trust that you will be okay?

Finding Your Ego: As I said, egos relish being right, even at the expense of sacred objects such as cherished relationships. There's a saying in psychotherapy that applies here: "You can be right, or you can be in a relationship." Create more awareness around the need to be right; you will find your ego there.

Mindful Bathing

15 minutes

Water has powerful healing properties, soothing our muscles, clearing out the old, and making space for the new. Despite this, many of us are on autopilot while we bathe, lost in ruminations of the past or thoughts about the future. When you bring mindfulness to your washing rituals, whether at the sink or in the shower or the bath, you tap into the healing power of water that is always available to you.

1. When you are washing your hands, dishes, or other objects throughout the day, be grounded in the present moment. Take some slow, deep breaths with long exhales, and feel the movement of your breath in your body. Feel the places your body contacts other surfaces, including the floor.

2. Now that you are firmly rooted in the present moment, pay attention to the feeling of water on your hands.

3. Stay present with the sensation of water on your skin. If your mind wanders to other subjects, gently and kindly return to what you are doing in the here and now.

4. Notice the smell of any soap and the sounds of washing, and watch the movement of water and soap.

5. Next time you take a shower or bath, make the intention to be present throughout the entire shower or bath before you begin.

6. Notice your hand turning on the water.

7. Stay present with the water as you adjust the temperature.

8. Notice when the water first hits the rest of your body. How does this feel?

9. Stay mindful as you go about your cleaning ritual. What are the sights, sounds, smells, and feelings?

10. If you find your mind wandering to the past or future, gently and kindly return your focus to the present moment. Commit to being present throughout the entire bathing ritual.

11. If you are in the bath or can take a couple more minutes in the shower, note any areas of tension in your muscles. Perhaps you are carrying tightness in your jaw muscles, the muscles of your neck, your back, or hamstrings. Stretch into these areas of tension and let the water melt away any stress or trauma. If you are in a bath and can stay for a long time, do so, alternating between stretching and submerging. With time you will also notice the tension in your mind washing away.

Soothing Smells: Staying present during washing rituals can be greatly facilitated by buying aromatherapy soaps. Choose hand, dish, hair, and body soaps with scents that soothe you. When you smell them as you go about the bathing rituals of your day, they will remind you to come back to the present moment.

Awareness of Aversion

The Buddha taught about three sources of suffering in life: aversion, craving, and confusion (sometimes translated as delusion or ignorance). In this stillness practice, you'll start by exploring how aversion is directly related to your suffering. By aversion, I mean being in conflict with some aspect of yourself or your world; another word for this is resistance. The habit of resistance is so very strong in many of us that we may not even be aware of how much of life we do resist. Therefore, much of this practice is about becoming more aware of how resistance manifests in your life.

1. Find a quiet place to write.

2. Use the following writing prompts to explore how aversion or resistance leads to suffering in your life and how you can build more awareness about these processes.

3. Resistance comes up in many forms. Some examples of resistance include dread, worry, tension, stress, anger, hatred, fear, judging, complaining, blaming, and fighting. Can you think of other forms of resistance? What are the most common ways that resistance comes up for you? What is a situation in your life right now that you notice a lot of internal resistance to?

4. This is one way of thinking about suffering: suffering = pain x resistance. Pain is inevitable in life; if you are human, you will have pain, both physical and emotional. There is no avoiding this. The helpful teaching in this equation is that your resistance to this pain (I don't want to experience this pain; when will this pain go away?) multiplies your suffering. Identifying and letting

go of resistance when you can (yes, I'm feeling this now; I'll sit with it because I know it is not permanent) therefore reduces your suffering.

5. When you shine the light of awareness on the resistance inside, you can begin to let it go. How are you wishing your life was different than it actually is? What are you resisting?

6. So many of us are filled with judgment toward ourselves and others. How are your expectations of yourself, others, or the world unkind?

7. When life gets hard, do you escape to your thoughts? How are these forms of thinking a kind of resistance to the present moment?

8. The opposite of resistance or aversion is acceptance—one of the seven principles of mindful stillness practice. How have you been working on acceptance? How can you strengthen your ability to bring acceptance to your interactions with others and with the world and be open and receptive to yourself?

Unconditional Self-Love: There's an old saying that what we resist, persists. Many of us have parts of ourselves that we dislike, wish we could change, or would like to just go away. When we instead open to and even embrace these parts of ourselves, they begin to heal.

Stillness before Sleep

Insomnia, nighttime anxiety, and many other sleep disorders are incredibly common and can have many detrimental effects on your health and ability to thrive. When you begin to incorporate more stillness into your bedtime routine, you bring more peace and calm to this very important time of your day. This brief intervention can produce huge rewards in your health, work, relationships, and creativity.

1. Plan to unplug from all devices and work at least 15 minutes before bedtime, but the more time the better. Put your phone, computer, work, TV, and/or iPad away.

2. When you physically put these away, commit to also letting go of thoughts of work, relationships, schoolwork, and any other pending life challenges. Ground yourself firmly in the present moment. This time is about preparing for restorative sleep. Let go of the day, and trust that you will deal with whatever is ahead when it arrives.

3. Use some form of aromatherapy to let your body know that it is safe and soothed. Lavender or mint lotion (or whatever scent is calming and pleasant for you), diffusing essential oils, or simply burning a candle or melting wax with a scent that calms are all good ideas.

4. Perhaps change into very comfortable pajamas or a cozy robe.

5. Stay present through all your evening washing rituals.

6. Practice some of your the techniques from Calm Breathing (page 36) for a few minutes.

7. Do five moving mountain pose sequences (page 34), either seated or standing, by inhaling as you lift your arms up to mountain pose and exhaling as you float your hands down to your side. Move slowly and intentionally. If your mind wanders to the events of today or tomorrow, simply note this and return your attention to the movement of your body and your breath in the here and now.

8. If you notice any tension in your muscles, do some gentle stretching.

9. Choose a seated stillness practice for five minutes. Some good options include Mindfulness of the Breath (page 30), Loving-Kindness Meditation (page 42), Awareness of Sense Perceptions (page 32), Awareness of Thoughts (page 44), and Awareness of Emotions (page 58).

10. When you end your seated practice, make your way to your bed. When you are ready for sleep, if you find your mind continues to think about a variety of things, bring your hands to your belly and feel your hands rise and fall with each breath. If your mind wanders, gently and kindly bring it back again.

Tools for Insomnia: If you are having trouble sleeping, be gentle with yourself about this. Paradoxically, the more you chase sleep, the harder it is to find. Turn the clocks away, and let go of counting the hours. Trust that your body is resting and will sleep when it needs to. If you continue to struggle, consult a physician.

Awareness of Craving

This stillness practice addresses another source of suffering—craving. Identifying craving in yourself can be more challenging than identifying aversion, because aversion can often be louder. Craving may be subtle and in many ways is rewarded by our consumer society. In this stillness practice, you will build awareness of how craving shows up in your life and how it leads to suffering.

1. Find a quiet place to write, and use the following writing prompts to build more awareness around craving and understand how it can lead to suffering.

2. Desire for nutrition, shelter, rest, and connection are important to everyone's well-being and survival, but we can quickly go overboard, and excessive desire or craving can leave us in a perpetual state of discontent. Craving can be intriguing and alluring, but as your mindfulness grows, you will see the truth of its pernicious nature. How does excessive desire trick you? Do you ever go overboard in your desire for food, alcohol, other substances, relationships, sex, TV, or other media? How does being lost in craving feel in your body, mind, and soul?

3. We spend so much of our lives living for an imagined future, and once we get to the next milestone, we quickly set a new goal. This does not mean you shouldn't have goals and work toward them, but the underlying structure of many craving thoughts goes something like this: "When I am/have/become/accomplish _____, I will be okay." If you don't pause to reflect on this dynamic, your entire life will pass you by. In what ways have you lived

primarily for a future goal? How have you tied up your worth in whether you accomplish a goal? How can you release your attachment to outcome and be grounded in your intention in the present moment?

4. What external objects, people, and roles do you believe you need to be okay or complete? Are there objects, people, and roles you believe you couldn't live without? How does this belief serve you?

5. The truth is that we are all okay right here, right now. You are complete. Nothing outside of you will ever give you lasting peace or happiness. Does this truth resonate with you? How so (or why not)?

6. Do you have fantasies that you spend a lot of time indulging? How are you missing your life in the present as you pursue those fantasies or ideals?

Moving from Concepts to Presence: Many of us are so focused on the idea of how we want our lives to unfold that we miss all the beauty that surrounds us in the present moment. As you notice and release craving and practice gratitude and generosity, you begin to access all the power and peace you have here and now.

Warming Up the Spine

10 minutes

Many people deal with back pain, stiffness, poor posture, arthritis, degenerative disc disease, and other problems associated with the spine. Your spine houses part of your central nervous system, and you are wise to invest some time and effort in the alignment, flexibility, and strengthening of the muscles, tendons, and ligaments that support your spine. In this stillness practice, you bring love and care to your back.

1. Read through all of the following instructions before beginning. You may also wish to look at photographs of these poses on my website, AMindfulMD.com. I recommend a yoga or exercise mat for this practice, but a thick towel will work, too.

2. Come down on all fours with your palms, your knees, and the tops of your feet on the floor and your hips stacked over your knees. You can also do this practice seated. If you are in a chair, place your palms on your knees. Inhale and bring your chest forward and your head up, broadening across your collarbone. This is the yoga position called cow. As you exhale, arch your back, let your head drop, and bring your shoulders forward. This is the yoga position called cat.

3. Continue, moving slowly with your breath, inhaling into cow, exhaling into cat, for five cycles of breath. Stay present with the sensations in your body.

4. Lower yourself down onto your belly with your body prone, flat against the floor. Put your palms facedown on the floor next to your shoulders, and press the tops of your feet down into the floor. As you inhale, lift your

head and chest off the floor; your elbows should still be bent at about a 45-degree angle. This is baby cobra pose. Breathe here. Gaze down at the floor to keep your spine long. Engage your quadriceps at the fronts of your thighs to lift your knees a few inches off the floor, if you can. Inhale in baby cobra, then exhale and lower yourself down to the floor. Inhale and move up to baby cobra, then exhale down to prone for five cycles of breath.

5. When you have finished your fifth cycle, remain prone. Inhale, then, as you exhale, gently push yourself up until you are kneeling. Settle down into the kneel so your calves are tucked under your thighs. Now, bring your knees wide toward the edges of your mat, turn your feet in a bit so your big toes are touching, and then press your hips back toward your heels. Lean all the way forward, and put your forehead on the floor. Reach your arms forward with your palms resting on the floor. You're now in child's pose. Inhale to lengthen your spine, then exhale and sink your hips farther back toward your heels, lengthening and releasing across your lower back. Continue to lengthen your spine toward the front of your space on your inhales and bring your hips back toward your heels on your exhales for a total of five breaths. If you are in a chair, you can do the chair forward fold from Introduction to Mindful Movement (page 34).

Strengthening Your Back: If you would like to build more strength in the muscles of your back, from tabletop position, raise your right arm and straighten it forward so your biceps is by your ear. Then reach your left leg back, toes flexed toward the floor. This is bird dog pose. After a few cycles of breath, move to the opposite side—left arm forward, right leg back.

Awareness of Confusion

In this stillness practice, we address another source of suffering—confusion. Confusion or delusion manifests when you don't see yourself, others, and your world as they truly are. We often carry our past, our cultural conditioning, and our expectations into the present, and this colors our ability to see the truth of what is happening here and now. Here, you will build awareness around the manifestation of confusion in your life and how it leads to suffering.

1. Find a quiet place to write and reflect on the following prompts.

2. Your cultural conditioning and your life experiences affect how you perceive the world around you. You form core beliefs about yourself, others, and the world that guide so many of your decisions and behavior. These core beliefs are often wholly or partly unconscious, but they exert so much power over the direction your life takes. Core beliefs are different for everyone, but often they are variations on being defective in some way; identifying as small, bad, unlovable, unable, unsuccessful, and/or unworthy are all common core beliefs, and there are also many others. What are your core beliefs about yourself? What are your core beliefs about others? How were they shaped, and how have they directed your life?

3. Your ego believes that you are independent and separate from everyone else. It is therefore focused on "What I want" and "What I need." The truth is that we are all interconnected and interdependent. At the most basic level, we couldn't survive without the oxygen in

our atmosphere, the water supplied to us through services maintained by other people, and the food that our Mother Earth grows and that other people farm, package, and bring to us. We are all a part of something so much larger than ourselves. How do you feel separate, afraid, and deficient? How are you connected to and interdependent with all life?

4. We confuse temporary pleasures, accomplishments, and relationships for true, lasting happiness. True, lasting happiness comes from a deep knowledge that you are whole and complete, just as you are, right here and now. What do you mistakenly look to for true, lasting happiness? How can you embrace the truth of your wholeness?

The Power of Clarity: If you could see the truth of who you really are—whole, loving, beautiful, and connected to all life—what kind of life would you create? What kind of power would you have to effect positive change in yourself and the world around you?

Stillness before Responding to Emails

10 minutes

Technology has made our lives easier in a lot of ways, but in some ways, technology brings more noise. One form of this noise is the barrage of emails that many of us get daily. Some of these emails can be particularly triggering, and you may have a habit of avoiding them or responding from a reactive place. In this practice, you will weave stillness into responding to emails.

1. Read through the following steps before the next time you plan to go through your emails, so you fully understand this exercise.

2. Before you open your inbox, pause for two to five minutes of seated or moving meditation.

3. Before opening any emails, ground yourself in your body and your breath.

4. Begin to go through your inbox, bringing mindfulness to any thoughts, emotions, or sensations that arise. If you come across any challenging or triggering emails, hold off on responding and bookmark them for later in this practice.

5. Respond to easier emails, continuing to be grounded in your body.

6. If, while going through your inbox, you get distracted by other ideas or tasks, note the distractions and return to your inbox.

7. Come back to any challenging emails that you identi-
fied in this practice, or address old emails that you may
have been avoiding. If you don't have any challenging
emails right now, return to this practice the next time
you receive one.

8. Read slowly through the challenging email, noting any
thoughts, sensations, or emotions that come up. Ground
yourself in your breath and your body. If you are feeling particularly triggered, do some Calm Breathing
(page 36), Awareness of Sense Perceptions (page 32),
and/or Releasing Tension in the Head and Neck (page 46).

9. When you have finished slowly reading the email,
pause. If you know how to respond in a wise and
thoughtful manner, do so now.

10. If you are feeling defensive or reactive, commit to a
longer pause before responding.

11. Do two to five minutes of Mindfulness of the Breath
meditation (page 30).

12. If you are now feeling more centered and able to
respond in a conscious way, do so.

13. If you continue to feel defensive or reactive, commit to a
longer pause before responding.

14. Consider journaling about the situation, or speak to a
trusted friend, spiritual counselor, or psychotherapist.
Commit to returning when you have more clarity.

The Power of a Pause: Viktor E. Frankl, a psychiatrist who survived
the Holocaust, said, "Between stimulus and response there is a
space. In that space is our power to choose our response. In our
response lies our growth and our freedom." As you learn to pause
in difficult situations, you build peace in your heart and your world.

Mindfulness in Household Chores

It's very easy to go on autopilot when you're doing chores. You can get lost in ruminations on the past, thoughts of the future, and worries about any number of things. In this practice, you bring stillness to chores, building the habit of present-moment awareness and strengthening the underlying neural networks that support mindfulness by stepping out of the concept of chores and becoming grounded in the experience. When you practice staying present in these basic ways, it becomes easier to stay present through difficult experiences. Begin with 15 minutes, and then slowly increase the time. I will start by discussing general considerations for all chores and then touch on a few different types of chores.

1. For this stillness practice, pick one chore and start with 15 minutes. Read all the way through the instructions before you begin.

2. Set aside a couple of moments before you start the chore to set the intention to stay present through-out the whole task. During the activity, whenever you find your mind drifting off somewhere else, note this departure and gently and kindly come back to the present moment.

3. When preparing and cooking meals, pause to note your intention to nourish yourself and/or your family. Notice the sounds, smells, flavors, temperatures, and textures of the food as you prepare it. Show up fully for the steps of making a meal, including washing, chopping, spreading, cutting, mixing, stirring, cooking, and seasoning.

4. When doing laundry, take extra care with the clothes. Notice the color, shape, and feel of the different garments.

5. When straightening, vacuuming, mopping, spraying, wiping, spreading, and performing other cleaning movements, notice the sights, the sounds, and the full range of movements in your body.

6. Yardwork can be particularly grounding, because being outside is healing. Feel the wind, temperature, and sunshine on your skin. Listen to the sounds around you, and fully feel the textures that you contact.

Practicing Beginner's Mind: You may not give household chores your full attention for a variety of reasons. One large reason is that because you have done similar activities so many times before, you don't believe there's anything new or worth paying attention to. But this is precisely the reason why chores are a beautiful opportunity to strengthen beginner's mind—one of the principles of mindfulness. Beginner's mind teaches that when you are fully in the present, there is unique richness to each and every moment, no matter how many times you may have done similar activities. Although the concept of chores can feel rote and stale, when you fully engage with the work before you, you discover that each moment is brand-new.

Self-Compassion with Difficult Emotions

5 minutes

Many of us respond to difficult emotions in ways that create more suffering. You may judge yourself and your experiences, get lost in unhelpful thinking, or escape to food, alcohol, TV, or other distractions. Even though your intention with these responses is to alleviate your pain, these habitual patterns only do more harm. When you instead practice showing up for yourself with kindness and compassion, you establish new neural networks that promote healing.

1. I recommend that you read through these instructions at least once when you are feeling relatively calm, and then refer back to them when you are dealing with difficult emotions, such as fear, anger, or sadness.

2. If you are flooded by very strong emotions, you may wish to do some Calm Breathing (page 36), Body Scan (page 38), Awareness of Sense Perceptions (page 32), or Introduction to Mindful Movement (page 34) exercises first.

3. Compassionate touch can soothe on multiple levels when you are overcome by difficult emotions. The touch releases oxytocin, a hormone that can calm you even when you are having difficulty calming down through other means. Compassionate touch can also be a way to communicate love and care for yourself. Try this by giving yourself a hug (wrap your arms around yourself), holding your own hand, placing both hands over your heart or your belly, or placing one hand over your heart and one hand on your belly. Hold this compassionate touch through the rest of the steps.

4. Acknowledge how you may have abandoned yourself during difficult times in the past, and apologize to yourself for any pain you may have caused.

5. Tell yourself that you promise to start showing up with compassion for yourself when you are in pain. Many of us are blessed to have people who love and care for us, but ultimately these people may leave your life. Make a vow to love and care for yourself throughout your entire life.

6. Make space for any difficult emotions that are present. Ground yourself in your body, and notice any sensations that are present.

7. Consider the most soothing thing someone could say to you in the midst of your pain. Perhaps "This will pass," "You are going to be okay," "I am here for you," or "I understand" would be a salve for your soul right now. If you are having difficulty with this, imagine a person in your life who is very comforting. What would you like them to say to you now? Say this to yourself.

Commit to a Self-Compassion Practice: As with any new skill, self-compassion takes practice. Just as you would commit to regular exercise to improve your fitness, commit to a regular self-compassion practice. In the beginning, this may feel awkward or even forced; that is 100 percent okay and to be expected. Don't give up on yourself.

Stillness in Relationships

15 minutes

As many of us who have been a part of nourishing spiritual communities know, practicing stillness with others can be profound. Meditating, praying, or discussing spiritual teachings with a community or even one other person can be incredibly supportive to your stillness practice. In this stillness practice, we start to explore the practice of stillness with others, and in future practices we will continue to look into other ways a stillness practice can nourish relationships.

1. Find at least one other person to try this with. In person is awesome, but if that isn't possible, feel free to use a teleconferencing platform such as FaceTime or Zoom.

2. Start with about five minutes of meditation or prayer. You don't necessarily need to both pick the same type of stillness practice, but this may support your practice. You may consider using a guided meditation, or one person may lead the others in the meditation by giving prompts if they feel comfortable doing so. Or feel free to practice together in silence.

3. After you have meditated for five minutes, gently return to the community.

4. Depending on the number of people present, allow some or all people to check in briefly on how the meditation was for them. What did you notice? Were there any challenges? As another is speaking, practice staying very present, listening carefully to their words.

5. As a group, choose a spiritual topic to discuss for the remainder of the time (10 minutes, and possibly longer if time allows). Feel free to choose a topic that we have

already covered in this book, such as becoming aware of the ego, aversion, craving, or confusion. You may also choose to jump ahead to topics covered in later stillness practices. If you are having difficulty getting started, read through a practice topic together, and instead of writing in a journal, as suggested for individual practice, use the questions as discussion prompts. Take turns answering the questions.

6. Practice being very present for one another. Be grounded in the sensations in your body, including the movement of your breath and the places where your body contacts other surfaces. When someone else is speaking, listen with your full attention. If you catch your mind wandering, gently and kindly come back to the present moment. While another person is speaking, if you feel compelled to say something, notice this urge and return to the act of listening.

The Gift of Presence: Staying very present when you are in community with others is such a powerful gift. Many of us tend to be thinking of what we would like to say while others are talking, and we may also have a tendency to interrupt. In your day-to-day life, practice listening to others with your full attention.

Street Loving-Kindness Meditation

10 minutes

In this practice, you bring loving-kindness meditation to the streets. When you are walking in public, you may tend to become lost in your mind, oblivious to the people you pass. Perhaps you feel very separate from or even frightened by the people you do not know. In this meditation, you practice being grounded in the present moment as you walk down the street, silently offering loving-kindness phrases to the people you come across.

1. Note: The following instructions refer to walking, but they can be easily adapted to any mode of transportation or movement.

2. The next time you plan to go walking in a place where there will be other people, read through the following instructions first. Write the following phrases (or any version that resonates deeply with your heart and soul) on a sheet of paper for reference, or commit them to memory:

    May I/you be safe and protected, free from internal harm and external threat.

    May I/you be physically healthy, vital, and full of life.

    May I/you be truly happy and deeply peaceful.

    May I/you live my/your life with ease.

3. If you need a refresher on this type of meditation, feel free to return to the Loving-Kindness practice on page 42.

4. Before you begin walking, ground yourself in the present moment. Take some slow, deep breaths with long, slow exhales. Feel the places your body contacts other surfaces and the movement of your breath in your body. Bring your attention to the sights, sounds, and smells around you. If you are feeling anxious or otherwise distressed, perhaps give yourself some compassion through soothing touch and a kind message of support. (See Self-Compassion with Difficult Emotions, page 78, for more information).

5. Start walking, and bring your attention to the sensations and the movement of your body in space. As you are walking, begin practicing loving-kindness meditation. I recommend that you repeat the phrases silently to yourself.

6. Start your practice by offering yourself loving-kindness as you walk down the street. Receive these loving messages from yourself.

7. When you have finished with yourself, begin silently offering the loving-kindness phrases to the people you pass.

8. Notice your internal reactions to this practice of offering these loving-kindness messages to the people you pass. How does it feel in the beginning? Does this feeling change at all with time or practice?

Creating Connection: Offering loving-kindness to people you do not know can help change your view of yourself, others, and the world. You move from feeling small, alone, separate, and afraid to feeling more connected to all beings everywhere and part of something much greater than yourself.

Awareness of Fear

We can become so used to fear that we do not even know it's there. As your stillness practice grows and you become more present for your internal experiences, the amount of fear inside you may be overwhelming. In this stillness practice, you will begin to slowly work through your fear. You do this by nurturing awareness of the fear and then letting go of it.

1. Find a quiet place to write and reflect on the following writing prompts.

2. There are many ways fear can manifest, including stress, anxiety, worry, obsessions, feeling overwhelmed, insecurity, ruminations, compulsions, panic, dread, and tension. How does fear show up for you?

3. When fear is present, you may try to fight or resist it; this resistance can cause you to suffer. Describe your resistance to fear. How can you make space for the fear, know that it doesn't define you, and trust that it will pass?

4. One of my favorite allegories for fearful behavior is a man who is constantly tapping, day and night. Another person observes this and asks why he is constantly tapping. The man responds, "I tap to keep the elephants away." The man had never stopped tapping long enough to see that no elephants came. Some people never stop their fearful behaviors (worrying, checking, questioning) long enough to see that not only are they okay without these behaviors, but in fact they are much better off than they think. These behaviors drain you of your energy, take you away from the present moment,

and erode your trust in yourself. What is your version of tapping? How can you create more awareness of these behaviors in your life?

5. As you build awareness of these fearful behaviors, you will become better able to catch yourself in the act or even notice the urge to act. Whenever you notice it, pause for a moment. You may notice your anxiety or discomfort begin to rise. Stay present with this, and, if you need to, do some Calm Breathing (page 36), Awareness of Sense Perceptions (page 32), Self-Compassion with Difficult Emotions (page 78), or Mindfulness of the Breath (page 30) practices. Ultimately, if you stay present and compassionate with yourself, the anxiety or discomfort will pass, and you will have the therapeutic experience of letting go of the patterns that reinforce fear in your life. How will you support yourself in pausing and letting go of fearful patterns?

Meditation on Fear: The Persian poet Hafiz wrote, "Fear is the cheapest room in the house. I would like to see you living in better conditions." Fear may be omnipresent, but you can empower yourself by building awareness around your fear, letting go of resistance, and releasing old, fearful behaviors that keep you locked in that cheap room.

Stillness on the Go

You spend a lot of time going from one place to another in life, but you can always bring your stillness practice with you. Whether you are biking, using public transportation, driving, or flying, practicing presence can help keep you grounded and give you an opportunity to reinforce these healing habits. I will begin by discussing general considerations for practice with all types of transportation, and then I'll touch on practices tailored to specific types of transportation.

1. For this stillness practice, pick one type of transportation, start with 15 minutes, and read through the instructions before you start.

2. Take at least a couple of moments (and possibly longer) before your journey to set the intention to practice stillness for at least 15 minutes of your journey. When your mind begins to wander during your practice, return your attention to the present moment.

3. Fear in some form around driving, flying, or public transportation is relatively common. If you are someone who has some anxiety around one or all of these modes of transportation, I recommend that you start with stillness practices that are more immediately calming, such as Calm Breathing (page 36), Awareness of Sense Perceptions (page 32), Self-Compassion with Difficult Emotions (page 78), or Mindfulness of the Breath (page 30). If your anxiety becomes particularly high, you may wish to practice these meditations before the trip so your skills and the underlying neural networks are strong.

4. For biking, feel the fresh air on your skin and notice the movements of your legs and your body through space. When your mind wanders, notice where it has wandered to. What thoughts typically consume you when you are on your bike? Then gently and kindly ground yourself in the pedaling and the world around you.

5. Public transportation is a beautiful opportunity to practice loving-kindness. Offer phrases of your own or the ones in the Street Loving-Kindness Meditation (page 82) to yourself, then to the people around you. Loving-kindness meditation can be a powerful antidote to fear and anger.

6. Pause the next time you get in your car or on a plane, and set your intention to practice stillness for 15 minutes. If you have anxiety driving or flying, let go of anxious thoughts, ground yourself in your body and your breath, and be gentle with yourself. Rather than judge or fight your driving or flying anxiety, make space for the entirety of your experience.

Addressing Anxiety: If you have anxiety about public buses or trains, driving, and/or flying, rather than avoiding these methods of transportation, practice grounding and self-compassion before and during your trips. Avoidance reinforces your fears and shrinks your comfort zone. If you continue to struggle even when you are using these tools, consider speaking to a mental health professional.

Awareness of Anger

Anger can be a very challenging emotion. You may get lost, stuck in, or consumed by anger, and it might cause you to act in ways that are not true to your values. However, like all emotions, anger is a messenger; in and of itself, it is not negative. Nurturing a strong stillness practice can help you build awareness of your anger, begin to peel away the layers, heed the message, and start the process of healing.

1. Find a quiet place to write and respond to the following prompts.

2. There are many variations of anger, including irritation, impatience, frustration, resentment, hatred, blame, and rage. How does anger come up for you?

3. Anger, like all emotions, gives you information about yourself, others, and the world. Are there situations in which anger helps you understand and address challenges in life?

4. Anger is often a secondary emotion that is fueled by other, more vulnerable emotions, such as fear or sadness. For example, when someone cuts you off in traffic, you are briefly scared and then quickly become angry. For many of us, anger feels more empowering than other difficult emotions. Understanding how anger can be a secondary emotion is important, because you learn that sometimes you need to dig a little deeper, and stillness practice is an excellent tool. What are some situations in your life where fear, sadness, or other emotions fuel your anger?

5. Many people who struggle with anger learned the habit from caregivers in childhood. How was anger modeled to you when you were small? Have you carried any of this anger with you on your life journey? Overreactions often indicate a historical component.

6. Your ego loves to stoke the fire of anger with its insistence on being right. Many of us tend to get lost in stories about how we are right and others are wrong. Anger thrives in black-and-white thinking like this. How can you practice noticing your ego in your attachment to being right?

7. When we react disproportionately with anger, we often become angry at ourselves. When you approach your anger this way, you are just layering anger on top of anger. Meet yourself instead with patience, kindness, and forgiveness. How do you fuel your anger? How can you shift this to a kinder approach?

Meet Anger with Loving-Kindness: Loving-kindness meditation is a powerful antidote to disappointment and fear, which can often fuel anger. When I find myself trapped in negative thoughts about a difficult person in my life, I practice loving-kindness meditation for this person, and the dissolution of anger always amazes me.

Sun Salutation

5 minutes

This moving meditation builds on the mindful movement you practiced earlier. In this sequence of yoga poses, you bow to the sun, the light that fuels our Mother Earth. The physical strength you develop from practicing sun salutations is inspiring, and can help you develop emotional and spiritual strength as well. If this kind of movement is challenging for you, skip this practice and concentrate on seated movements, such as Introduction to Mindful Movement (page 34).

1. You may wish to practice in front of a window that faces the sun. Read through these instructions first before beginning. You may also wish to look at photographs of these poses at my website, AMindfulMD.com.

2. Standing at the front of a mat or towel with your palms pressed together, thumbs at your sternum (heart center)—the yoga pose standing at attention. Close your eyes, or soften your focus and lower your gaze. Choose an intention for your practice. If you cannot think of one, I offer my own intention of developing physical, emotional, and spiritual strength.

3. Inhale as you raise your arms up over your head to mountain pose.

4. Exhale and fold forward at your hips, with a small bend in your knees, and reach your arms toward the floor—the yoga pose forward fold.

5. Inhale and straighten your back, creating an inverted L with your body, bringing your palms to your thighs and broadening across your collarbones—the yoga pose halfway lift.

6. Exhale as you move down to plank pose (the top of a push-up) with your shoulders aligned over your wrists and your hips in a horizontal line with your shoulders. If you need more support, drop your knees to the floor.

7. Inhale in plank pose, and as you exhale, lower your body to lie flat on the floor, keeping your palms on the floor just outside of your shoulders. Press the tops of your feet down into the floor. On your inhale, lift your head and chest off the floor into baby cobra pose (your elbows should be bent at about 45 degrees). As you exhale, lower yourself back down to lying flat with your palms still flat on the floor just outside of your shoulders. Inhale here.

8. Tuck your toes, exhale as you straighten your arms, and push your sit bones back and up toward the sky, creating an inverted V shape with your body. This is the yoga pose downward-facing dog. If you are new to yoga, you may wish to move from lying flat to on your hands and knees with a flat back and then into downward dog.

9. Inhale and look forward. Exhale and step to the front of your mat with your hands still on the floor.

10. Inhale and move into halfway lift.

11. Exhale into forward fold.

12. Inhale to mountain pose.

13. Exhale as you stand at attention.

Yoga for Your Health: Sun salutations are a beautiful practice in the morning before meditating. If you are enjoying mindful movement, perhaps consider a yoga asana class to further deepen your practice. Yoga practice not only helps your posture, flexibility, and strength, but it can also be tremendously grounding and help with depression, anxiety, and PTSD.

Awareness of Sadness

10 minutes

In this human life, sadness is unavoidable. You cannot escape loss in its many forms, and sadness is a natural response to this loss. Some of us are conditioned to either get lost in our sadness or resist it. Mindfulness practice enables you to take the middle way, becoming present for your sadness in a kind and non-judgmental way, ultimately serving your healing and transformation as well as your connection to others.

1. Find a quiet place to write and reflect on the following prompts.

2. Sadness, like all emotions, comes in many shapes and forms, including disappointment, shame, guilt, despair, agony, grief, sorrow, depression, helplessness, and hurt. How does sadness come up for you?

3. We all face loss throughout our lives. This can be loss of relationships, roles, beliefs, jobs, health, abilities, loved ones, and ultimately our life. Sadness and grief are natural responses to these losses. How have you faced loss in your life, and have you been able to iden-tify, understand, express, and process your sadness or grief? What losses have you had difficulty facing? How can grieving these losses help you heal and transform?

4. Do you either get lost in sadness or resist it? What are your core beliefs related to sadness? Some of us learned that we are unable to move past sadness. Others were conditioned to associate sadness with weakness. We may have a pattern of suppressing sadness or quickly covering it over with anger or other distractions. How does your conditioning shape your relationship with sadness?

5. Shame—feeling as if you are bad, wrong, defective, unlovable, and/or small in some way—is often considered a secondary emotion, and some people who study emotions believe sadness is the primary emotion that drives shame. Also, deep feelings of intense shame can contribute to feeling sad and/or depressed. Shame tends to thrive in silence. Are there any ways that you struggle with shame? When you shine the light of awareness on shame, either through journaling or through speaking with a psychotherapist, spiritual counselor, or trusted friend, you begin to see shame loosen up and dissolve.

6. Grieving (which involves turning inward and expressing sadness) the care you deserved and didn't receive as a child is key to healing. What care did you deserve but not receive as a child, and how can you give this care to yourself now?

7. You experience sadness, like all emotions, in your body. Where do you feel sadness in your body? What does it feel like?

Strengthening Connections: Expressing sadness in the context of kind, attentive relationships can deepen your connection to others. If you can use mindfulness and self-compassion to create space for both the sadness you experience and the sadness of others in your life, you will benefit from deeper, more meaningful relationships.

Stillness with Children

A powerful way to create more peace here on Earth is to show up with your full, kind presence for the children in your life. These children may be your family, friends, neighbors, or even children you encounter through volunteer or paid work. Children have so much to teach us, and we are wise to listen. When you model stillness to children, you teach the next generation a more peaceful way to live.

1. Set a timer and plan to spend 15 minutes with a child without distractions, including your phone and other electronics like a TV, computer, or iPad.

2. Set the intention to commit your full, undivided attention to the child for the next 15 minutes.

3. If the child wants to share a toy or a story with you, give them your full attention and delight in them. Stay grounded in the present, and show up fully. Listen with your entire being, and notice and pause when you sense the impulse to correct or interrupt. Reflect back what you hear the child sharing with you, and ask questions to understand further what they are expressing.

4. If the child is looking to you for direction during this time, perhaps recommend a toy, game, or story that you believe they will enjoy.

5. Laughing, roughhousing, and full-body movement are deeply healing for children. Maybe make the child into a taco or burrito with blankets and stuffed animals, or play a game where they must keep you from getting to the couch or bed. Let them win!

6. If the child expresses big emotions, such as anger, fear, or deep sadness, pause and notice any reactions within yourself. When you were small, you might have been taught that big emotions were bad or even danger-ous. Even though many of these emotional memories are largely, if not completely, unconscious, they can be quickly activated when you are an adult and the children around you experience big emotions. When unconscious emotional memories are activated, you may feel strongly compelled to quickly discourage or even shut down the feelings. Pause and notice this if it comes up for you. Ground yourself in your body, take some deep breaths with long, slow exhales, and if you are feeling triggered, offer yourself some self-compassion. Once you feel more grounded and calm, show up for the child and create space for their big emotions.

Modeling Stillness: Invite the children in your life to come and meditate and do yoga with you. They may only be able to meditate for a short period of time (a good rule is one minute for every year of life), and you may need to find a family yoga class (in person or online), but learning these practices early will help them through-out their lives.

Embracing Your Inner Child

Many of us have a hurt child inside ourselves who desperately needs our love, but for a variety of reasons we may have difficulty showing up for this inner child. Some form of disconnect or trauma in childhood created this wounded inner child, and we tucked them away deep inside our psyche, either because we were ashamed or because the pain was just too much to bear. Here, you practice returning to your hurt inner child with kind and loving presence.

1. Find a quiet place to write and meditate as you consider the following questions. If you notice any emotions come up while you are writing, I recommend that you pause, stop writing, and become grounded in your body and breath. Where do you notice the emotions? How do they feel? Stay patient and present with your emotions. Perhaps consider practicing some self-compassion. If you feel ready to return to the practice, do so. If at any point this practice feels too overwhelming or painful to deal with on your own, pause and ground yourself in the here and now. Grounding, self-compassion, mindful movement, walking meditation, or yoga may be therapeutic. When you feel ready, you may wish to bring this insight to a spiritual counselor, psychotherapist, or trusted friend.

2. You may notice your hurt inner child when you feel triggered or are experiencing big emotions. When you overreact to situations in your life, your hurt inner child may be closer to the surface. What types of situations are very difficult for you? Bring these to mind with as much detail as possible. Are there parts of yourself that

you feel ashamed of? Are there parts of yourself that feel traumatized? If you feel comfortable, write from these parts of yourself. What does your inner child want to say to you?

3. This is the heart of the practice, so please dedicate plenty of time for this step. Set your writing aside, read through this step, and then close your eyes if you feel comfortable doing so. Imagine that you could visit your hurt inner child. What do they look like? Where are they? Imagine that you, in your older and wiser state, walk right over to your hurt inner child and embrace them. What do you want to say to them? Tell your inner child that they have deep, inherent, and absolute worth and that they deserve unconditional love. Promise to continue to show up for them.

Becoming Whole: When you embrace all of yourself, even the parts that you're ashamed of or overwhelmed by, you begin to integrate and heal. When your hurt inner child feels more loved and accepted, you become whole. If this practice resonated with your heart, I recommend that you practice the visualization in step 3 regularly.

Gratitude Practice

Practicing gratitude is a powerful stillness method that can elevate your consciousness. We humans evolved with a strong negativity bias, because our ancestors who focused on present dangers survived and passed down these genes. Now that we don't have saber-toothed tigers and looming starvation as imminent threats, the evolutionary tendency to zoom in on everything wrong in our lives serves only to negatively affect our mental health. Gratitude is a powerful antidote to this negativity.

1. Find a quiet place to write and reflect on the following prompts.

2. We tend to focus on what's wrong with ourselves, others, and the world. Particularly with yourself, you may zoom in on your perceived deficits and all the work you want to do to address these deficits. Gratitude takes the opposite approach. What is right, right now? Starting with health, are any of your organs working? Even if you deal with health issues or limitations, do you enjoy any measure of health? Perhaps your liver is filtering your blood, or your heart is pumping blood all throughout your body.

3. What are you good at? Nothing is too simple. For example, do you give good hugs? Do you ever smile or hold the door for others? Do you work hard? Are you good at resting when you need to?

4. Some of us have qualities that we may minimize because our society or culture doesn't value them. Are you highly sensitive to others' emotions? Do you have body positivity? Do you take pride in your work, even if you don't make a lot of money?

5. What else is right, right now? Do you have a warm place to sleep? Do you have clothes and health care? Do you have anyone who loves or supports you? Do you have food to nourish your body? Write down everything you are grateful for that comes to mind.

6. What are you grateful for with the people closest to you? What are they good at? Even if they struggle with certain difficulties, do they have other strengths?

7. What about things that seem smaller? Perhaps a ray of sunshine through your window or a warm beverage? Or maybe a quiet morning or afternoon?

8. What about your community, city, state, or country? What are the good things about where you live?

9. What is good about humanity, past or present?

Gratitude Journal: Keeping a daily gratitude journal is a huge investment in your well-being. Even if you just jot down daily on your phone three things that you are grateful for, this can nourish your emotional and spiritual health. When you invest in yourself, you experience more stillness in your mind, heart, and soul.

Stillness in Shopping

15 minutes

Whether you are shopping for clothes, groceries, household items, gifts, or something else, everyone spends a fair amount of time in stores. Some people enjoy shopping, others could go either way, and some people really dislike shopping. Whatever category you fall into, when you bring your stillness practice to this everyday activity, you become more intentional in your day-to-day life and strengthen the neural circuitry that builds a foundation of peace and calm in your body.

1. The next time you go shopping, plan to practice still-ness for 15 minutes and set a timer. Read through these instructions before you begin.

2. Before you enter the store, set an intention to stay present for the entire 15 minutes. You may also wish to set an intention about what you want to accomplish with your shopping trip. If there are specific items you need to purchase, bring them to mind or jot them down on your phone or a piece of paper. If you just want to look around and you don't want to buy anything, you may wish to commit to this.

3. Get grounded in your body. Notice the floor underneath you and the movement of breath in your body. If you have anxiety about going into a store, take some extra time to ground yourself in all sense perceptions—sight, sound, smell, and touch. Practice self-compassion or some calm breathing techniques to help alleviate anxiety.

4. Enter the store slowly, and look all around you. What do you see? Who is there? What do you hear? What do you smell?

5. As you move, bring your attention to the movement of your body through space. Continue to look around you and move intentionally.

6. If your mind wanders, note this and kindly and gently return to the present moment.

7. Offer loving-kindness phrases to yourself and the people around you.

8. If you are selecting items, do so intentionally, noticing the movement of your hand and the textures of the items.

9. If you get distracted from your initial intention and find that you want to purchase other items that you may not need or that may not be healthy for your body, pause. Get grounded in your body, take some deep breaths, and return to your intention. If you continue to be unsure, you may wish to take a longer pause before continuing your shopping.

Online Shopping: Modify this practice for online shopping. Set your timer and an intention to stay grounded in your body. Before you begin, be clear about what you want to purchase. If at any point you find that your mind has wandered from these intentions, pause and come back to your intentions.

Work-Life Balance

Many of us have an old habit of tying up our worth with what we accomplish and/or what we earn. This habit can drive you to prioritize work, school, and other projects over your health, well-being, relationships, and other important areas of your life that you also highly value, such as spirituality and creativity. In this practice, you will slow down and begin to investigate your attitudes and behaviors around balancing work with the rest of your life.

1. Find a quiet place to write, set a timer for 15 minutes, and reflect on the following prompts.

2. So many people have difficulty unplugging from work. With more and more people working from home, boundaries between being on and off the clock have been further blurred, and many feel they are dealing with burnout, depression and/or anxiety. Do you have difficulty establishing boundaries between work and the rest of your life?

3. Many of us have difficulty living for today and are always working toward future career and financial goals. If you're not careful, you can spend your whole adult life focused on acquiring more status, accomplishments, and money. When age or illness finally starts to slow you down, you may not have the health and abilities that you had when you were younger to pursue your true passions and dreams. What is calling out to your heart right now? How can your stillness practice help you find joy right here and now?

4. Many people think they do not have time to exercise, eat healthy foods, and get needed medical care because they are too busy with work and other responsibilities. Some people neglect family, friends, their spiritual lives, and/or creativity because of work. Does any of this happen with you? What do you value in life?

5. Some people are on a constant quest for more money, and no amount ever feels like enough. A lot of happiness research has shown that once basic needs like food, clothing, shelter, and health care are met, more money doesn't equal more happiness. Also, people who are dying usually don't wish they had worked more or made more money. Most people regret spending too much time at the office, missing out on time with their families and friends, and not following their true passions. At the end of your life, what do you think will be important to you? How can you make that happen today?

Building a More Equitable World: Unfortunately, poverty is a reality for far too many people across the world, even in countries with plenty of resources. Some people must work long hours just to afford basic necessities. As we build mindfulness around desire, money, and other resources, we all contribute to a more equitable planet.

Balancing Postures

Working on your balance can build muscle tone, improve flexibility, reinforce proper alignment, and help prevent falls as you age. Balancing postures can also be very meditative, because they require a very high degree of focused attention for a stretch of time. Holding these postures can test your endurance and resilience as you shake, become uncomfortable, fall out of the poses, and decide to get back in again. This is another way to put the idea of beginning again into practice. If this kind of movement is too challenging for you, then skip this practice and concentrate on seated movement, such as Introduction to Mindful Movement (page 34).

1. I recommend an exercise or yoga mat for this practice. Read through these instructions first before beginning. You may also wish to look at photographs of these poses on my website, AMindfulMD.com.

2. Stand at the top of your mat with your feet separated by the width of your hips.

3. Come into tree pose on the right side. Keep your left foot flat on the floor and place your right sole somewhere along your left leg, avoiding your knee. Distribute your weight evenly into the sole of your left foot. If you are new to this practice or struggle with balance, you can keep your right toes on the floor and place the sole of your right foot on the inside of your left ankle.

4. Move your right knee back a bit, opening through your right hip. If you feel relatively stable, you may wish to move the sole of your right foot higher up on your left leg, perhaps to your calf or even your thigh, using your hand as needed.

5. When you feel relatively steady, press your palms together in front of your chest in heart center. Find a stable object in front of you that you can focus your gaze on, to help you maintain your balance. If you feel steady here, try bringing your hands to a different position, perhaps above your head like tree branches or even with your palms coming together behind your back.

6. Stay in tree pose for 10 to 20 seconds, about three to eight breaths. If you fall out of the pose before time is up, come right back in.

7. When you are done on the right, move to the left side and hold tree pose for another 10 to 20 seconds.

8. As you continue to practice, you can aim for a minute on each side. You may wish to place a clock with a second hand in front of your space.

Building Strength: Shaking and discomfort mean you are building muscle; breathe through both and maintain your gaze on your unmoving object. Continue practicing so you can stretch the time you spend in tree pose. Pain, however, means you should release the posture and consult with a yoga teacher, a physical therapist, or even a physician.

Media Reflection

The content that you read, watch, and listen to can powerfully affect your level of consciousness. Some of us are more sensitive than others, but we are all affected by the media we consume. Nurturing mindfulness about media consumption and exploring how the news, TV, videos, movies, and social media affect your sensing, thinking, and feeling can help you become more discriminating about what, when, and how much media you engage with.

1. Find a quiet place to write and reflect on the following prompts.

2. There seems to be a daily barrage of horrible stories in the news, and you can easily get drawn into wanting to know all the details. Some politicians or hot-button issues may be particularly triggering, and you may feel your stress levels rise as you read, listen to, or watch the news. You are wise to balance your need to be informed with your general well-being. What do you notice in your body, thoughts, and feelings when you are reading/listening to/watching certain triggering news stories? Is your stress response more amplified if you are watching news or if you are reading it? How well do you balance staying informed with taking care of yourself emotionally and spiritually? How can you practice being grounded in your body when you are engaging with challenging news stories?

3. Some of us may struggle with anger, and the media we consume can stoke this anger. With the polarization of politics, you can easily get lost in black-and-white thinking, believing you and those who think like you are the

"good" people and "they" are the bad people. Do you ever fall prey to this kind of thought? Is it possible that your ego becomes activated and needs to be right and make others wrong? How is this type of thinking not the whole story?

4. Some people notice that engaging with certain media content before bed affects their sleep or dreams in a negative way. Others notice that frightening shows or movies make their anxiety worse and/or that sad or depressing media creates more despair. Do certain types of media negatively affect you? Does the time of day matter?

5. What type of media lifts your spirits or resonates deeply with your heart? For many people, comedies, love stories, or spiritual stories can fill up their cups. Are there other types of media that feed your soul?

Social Media Health: Your engagement with social media can have very powerful effects on you. What pages, people, or accounts do you like or follow, and how do their posts usually affect you? Are there certain pages or accounts you can follow that will support your emotional, physical, and spiritual health?

Hip Opening

Your hips are the largest joints in your body, and therefore you may store a lot of tension and trauma there. Tight hip flexors can also result from a lot of sitting, running, or cycling and can contribute to lower-back pain. Yoga poses that help open the hips allow you to begin to release this tension and trauma and build better pelvic alignment that supports healthy posture.

1. Read all the way through these instructions before beginning. You may also wish to look at photographs of these poses on my website, AMindfulMD.com.

2. Start standing with your feet wider than your hips, toes turned out to the sides at a 45-degree angle. Slowly bend your knees, bringing your sit bones as close to the floor as possible and keeping your knees wide and the soles of your feet flat on the floor. This is frog squat pose. Feel free to rest your sit bones on a pillow or cushion or place a towel or fold your mat under your heels for more support. Breathe here. If frog squat pose is difficult, you may wish to try supine bound angle pose, where you lie on your back and bring the soles of your feet together, knees opened wide; you can rest one hand on your heart and one hand on your belly.

3. Come to forward fold—stand up and fold forward at your hips, with your forehead as close to your legs as is comfortable and your arms reaching toward the floor. Plant your palms flat on the floor, step your left foot back into a low lunge, and then drop your left knee to the floor. Inhale and lift your arms up to the sky for kneeling crescent pose. Place your hands at the front of your right thigh, and sink your hips forward to feel

a stretch along the front of your left hip flexors. Stay and breathe here. Imagine on your inhale that you are sending rich, oxygenated blood to the fibers of your left hip flexor, and on your exhale that you are releasing tension. Come back to kneeling crescent, then step your left foot up to meet your right foot so you are back in forward fold. Step your right foot back to low lunge, then follow the same steps you did on the other side. If you have difficulty coming into kneeling crescent, you can lie on your back and place a pillow underneath your sacrum to elevate your hips and stretch through your hip flexors.

4. Lie on your back on the floor or on a mat, and place your feet flat on the mat with your knees pointing up to the sky. Bring your right ankle up to rest on your left knee for supine figure-four pose. If this feels like a good stretch along the outside of your right hip, stay here and breathe into this area. If you would like to deepen your stretch, begin to slowly pull your left thigh or shin in closer to your chest. Repeat on the other side.

Healing Hip Poses: Bringing mindfulness to the sensations and emotions that come up while you are opening your hips can be very healing. There are many other hip-opening yoga asana poses, so if you enjoyed and benefited from this practice, you may wish to explore more of them.

Forgiveness Practice

The practice of forgiveness allows you to purify your heart by letting go of anger and resentment. Forgiveness doesn't necessarily mean that you need to condone or forget the harm that was done to you or that you need to have a relationship with the person who harmed you. Forgiveness means finding freedom from the negative energy in your heart after you have suffered harm by another.

1. Find a quiet place to sit and write, and read through these instructions before you begin.

2. First, spend a couple of minutes creating a list of all of the harms that you hope to someday forgive. Perhaps you didn't have the loving childhood you deserved, or a romantic partner hurt you, or someone betrayed or traumatized you. Write a list of the abuse, neglect, abandonment, harm, and violence you have suffered.

3. Choose one harm from this list that you would like to work on today. Start with a harm that doesn't feel like the most impossible to forgive—perhaps a 6 on a scale of 1 to 10.

4. Without censoring yourself, write everything that comes to mind about this harm. What happened, and how do you feel now? Is rage, disgust, hatred, a desire for vengeance, shame, resentment, sadness, grief, guilt, or suffering present? Pause for a moment and feel these emotions in your body. Where are the emotions? Describe how they feel. Can you give them a color? Tears and expressing emotions are healing, so allow

them to come if you feel safe. If any of the feelings are too strong, pause to practice some self-compassion, grounding, or calming breath.

5. If you wish to, reflect on the suffering that may have caused this person to harm you. It is completely okay to skip this step if it's too much right now.

6. Dedicate plenty of time for this visualization. Close your eyes if that feels comfortable, and imagine the person you would like to forgive. What do you want to say to this individual? If you feel ready, you may wish to communicate your intention to forgive them. In other words, you are ready to release the negative energy of this harm from your heart. If you do not yet feel ready to forgive, that is 100 percent okay. Imagine a healing and cleansing light bathing your heart and freeing you from all the negative energy associated with this hurt. Visualize a peaceful light embracing your entire being.

7. Can you offer yourself forgiveness? If you are carrying anger at yourself for past wrongs, do this same practice for yourself. Maya Angelou explains it beautifully: "Do the best you can until you know better. Then when you know better, do better."

Creating Safety: If any of the emotions feel too overwhelming to face on your own, practice self-compassion, grounding, mindful movement, and calming breath, set aside the practice, and commit to picking it up again with a trusted friend, spiritual counselor, or therapist. Write a letter to the person if you believe it will help you heal. You don't need to send it if you don't want to.

Moving in the Direction of Love

What would you like to create in your life? Are there any creative goals you would like to work toward? Perhaps you want to draw, paint, write, photograph, film, record, illustrate, design, bake, cook, create, code, build, redesign, renovate, or do something entirely different. Do you have other types of goals that are pulling at your heartstrings: perhaps to find a partner, have a family, work in a particular field, or start a business?

1. Find a quiet place to write and reflect on the following prompts.

2. What kind of creative pursuits have you enjoyed in your life? Is there something you have always wanted to try? Is there a class you have wanted to take? Or maybe even a program or a degree you want to pursue that you have been putting off?

3. What are your dreams and passions? What do you want more than anything else?

4. What is stopping you from pursuing your goals? How is fear holding you back? What are you afraid of? Are you concerned that you will not be good enough? Or that it will be too difficult or too expensive? Write down all your fears.

5. Now imagine your fears are guests that often come to your house. Normally they knock on your door, and you immediately let them in and give them free rein of the whole house. They are obnoxious guests, and you entertain them all day even though you would rather be spending your time doing other things you enjoy more.

In the past you have allowed your fears to call the shots and decide how you spend your time. Rather than succumb to or fight or judge your fears, can you allow them to be present, perhaps offer them a hot beverage, and continue about your day? Let them know that you are busy and you are unable to entertain them.

6. Are these truly your fears, or is it possible you have internalized the fears of someone else in your life? Can you visualize this person and let them know that you are safe and you do not need to carry around these fears any longer?

7. Can you decide to live your life motivated by love, curiosity, creativity, inspiration, or other forces much more powerful than fear?

8. What small step toward your goals can you commit to today?

Making Space: You can learn to allow your fear to be present but limit the extent to which it is driving the direction of your life. Cultivate mindfulness of fear throughout your day, noticing when it is present and the impulse to follow its advice. Acknowledge your fear and say, "No, thanks. I choose love."

Practicing with Conflict

Conflict with other people in your life can activate past inter-personal trauma that you previously internalized. If you do not become aware of when this happens, you may carry your past trauma into your current relationships. Your intention may be to protect yourself from being hurt in the same way you have been before, but unfortunately, this ultimately does not serve you. In this practice, you will build awareness of your fear and then work toward healing.

1. Find a quiet place to write and reflect on the following prompts.

2. What past interpersonal trauma is being activated inside of you now, in your current relationships? Were you abandoned, hurt, abused, neglected, betrayed, ignored, or objectified? Write about the trauma that happened to you in the past that continues to affect you now.

3. Although this may not be fully conscious, when your old pain is triggered in conflicts with others, you become afraid that the harm you suffered in the past will happen again. This fear activates your sympathetic nervous system, the part of the autonomic nervous system that is responsible for fight, flight, and freeze. When you are afraid, do you typically feel the impulse to fight or flee, or do you freeze? What does this look like for you? Although acting on your impulse to fight or flee may temporarily bring down your fear, it unfor-tunately reinforces this entire fear pattern and causes you suffering in the long term. If you can instead

practice showing up for yourself with love and compassion when these past traumas are activated in conflict, you can begin to heal and release your old fears.

4. Read through the remaining steps first and then proceed. Close your eyes and bring to mind a recent conflict in which you believe this old traumatic dynamic was activated. Recall as many of the details as possible. If writing about the conflict helps you bring up the associated emotions, please do this. Write freely, letting go of any desire to censor yourself.

5. Notice any difficult emotions that may have come up for you. What are they? Can you describe them?

6. If any difficult emotions come up, practice showing up for yourself with love and kindness. Perhaps do some self-compassion, grounding, mindful movement, yoga, or calming breath.

7. Promise to pause and practice these same acts of love for yourself the next time you feel triggered in a conflict.

Healing Compassion: When you experience difficult emotions during conflict, can you pause and show up for yourself with love and compassion and be present with, instead of acting out, the urge to lash out or run away? In this way you heal your old hurts and prevent them from causing further harm.

Open Awareness

In earlier practices, you built awareness around your sensations, thoughts, and emotions. Now you will put them all together in this open-awareness meditation. In contrast to earlier practices where you focused on just one thing that you gently returned to whenever your focus strayed, with open awareness you pay singular attention to whatever comes into your awareness. Having the object of your focus shift during the practice can be particularly challenging when you are starting out, so please be kind and patient with yourself.

1. Find a quiet place to practice that is relatively free of distractions. Read through all the instructions before you begin.

2. In contrast to other meditations where you invest effort to keep your focus on one object and release all other objects, here you let go of any task or assignment and rest in open awareness. In this way, during open-awareness meditation you shift from doing to being.

3. Sit in an upright and comfortable posture that fosters wakefulness.

4. Set your timer for 10 minutes.

5. Close your eyes if that feels comfortable, or lower your gaze and soften your focus.

6. Take a couple of deep breaths with long, slow exhales.

7. Return to your natural breath rhythm.

8. Open your awareness to any object—sensation, thought, or emotion—that enters it. Whatever it is, give it all your attention and examine it with curiosity and no judgment.

9. Practice being open and receptive to anything that comes into your awareness. Stay with the object fully while it is present, and then release it as it floats by and a new object enters your awareness.

10. Notice all the sensations that come into awareness, whether touch, sound, taste, smell, or sight. Remain open like the sky, as if the objects are clouds floating through you.

11. Stay present with the thoughts that enter your awareness, regardless of the content of the thoughts. Release any impulse to judge or understand the thoughts, and simply bear witness to them while they remain in awareness.

12. Open to any emotion that enters your awareness, be with it fully while it is present, and then release it as it leaves.

13. If you notice that you are struggling with this meditation, open to the experience of struggling. Be with any confusion, frustration, boredom, or sleepiness that may arise. Watch how your experience changes over time.

14. When your timer goes off, slowly come back into your body and open your eyes.

Deep Peace: When you regularly practice resting in open awareness—witnessing all objects as they arise and fall away and letting go of any agenda—you build a large reserve of internal peace and equanimity. Then, when difficult situations arise in your life, you are able to draw on this deep peace and equanimity.

Awareness of Interdependence

We touched on this principle in the practice Awareness of Confusion (page 72), and here we further explore interdependence. Interdependence teaches you that you rely on other people, other beings, and many other conditions for everything—from your very existence to all the ways you are able to thrive. When you explore this principle, you see that we are not as separate as we seem but are really a part of something so much bigger than ourselves.

1. Find a quiet place to write and reflect on the following prompts.

2. What do Mother Earth and the beings on it provide to you that you need to survive? Who else contributes to the basic things you need to survive? Who helps bring clean water, electricity, and gas to your home?

3. Who was involved in making your home? How were your clothes made, and who was involved? What other items in your home do you need? How were they created, where did you purchase them, and how were they brought to you?

4. What type of food do you eat, and how was it grown or cared for? What did these living organisms depend on to live? Who brought the food to where it was purchased? Who shops and/or brings the food to your home? Who prepares it? Who cleans your home?

5. Are there any medicines or other medical treatments that you and your family depend on? Who cares for your physical and mental health?

6. Who cared for you when you were a newborn, infant, toddler, preschooler? Where did you go to school, and who contributed to your school and your education? Did you play sports or do any other activities? Who was involved? Who took care of you?

7. What type of transportation do you use, and who operates it? Who helped build these modes of transportation? What were they made from, and how are they maintained? Who and what is involved in maintaining the roads you use?

8. Is anyone else involved in caring for or educating your family members?

9. Are you a part of any spiritual or social communities?

10. Do you work, or does anyone in your family work? If so, who and what is needed for your/their job?

11. Who contributes to the safety, security, health, and maintenance of your community, city, state, country, and world?

12. Who and what else is essential to your life and well-being?

Connection: Even though it can sometimes feel as if you are all alone, you can set the intention to regularly reflect on all of your connections to all beings everywhere. When you regularly reflect on your interdependence, you begin to feel much more connected to the universe, your planet, and all of life everywhere.

Cultivating Contentment

In this practice, we'll work toward living from a place of deep, unconditional contentment that is not dependent on any outside circumstances. As you have previously seen, your ego feels separate, deficient, and persistently unsatisfied. When you live from your ego, true, lasting happiness and deep contentment are perpetually elusive. Here, you practice resting in a place free of grasping and craving, which enables you to experience lasting contentment and equanimity.

1. Find a quiet place to write and reflect on the following prompts.

2. As you learned in the Awareness of Ego practice (page 60), your ego feels small, defective, attached to being right, and constantly wanting more. When you live rooted in your ego, what is your experience? Do you experience deep contentment and happiness? Feel free to return to the practice on ego to get a better sense of your experience of your ego.

3. Your ego often reaches for pleasure, gain, praise, and fame and pushes away their opposites: pain, loss, blame, and disrepute. But unfortunately, life contains all these things, the good and the bad, and this resistance leads to suffering. How do these opposites come up in your life? How do they affect you? How can you make space for all of life as it unfolds and not let it affect your self-love, peace, and happiness?

4. You can build equanimity by resting deep down in your unconditional self-love and regard. If you compare your life to the ocean, life can be very chaotic

and tumultuous when storms rage on the surface. If you stay on the surface, or at the level of the ego, you can be thrashed about and feel perpetually insecure and discontented. If you instead dive down below the surface, you can access a deep reserve of peace and stillness that is not affected by what is happening above. Close your eyes now and visualize yourself resting in the deep inner peace and contentment of your self-acceptance. Give yourself a hug and know that here you cannot be harmed by your outside circumstances and conditions.

It's All in You: When life gets hard, picture yourself dropping below your outer circumstances, giving yourself a hug or squeezing your hands, and resting in your unconditional self-love and regard. Understand that your self-worth doesn't depend on anything external to you, and promise to always remember this and continue to show up for yourself.

Restorative Yoga

In restorative yoga, also called yin yoga, healing poses are held for longer periods of time for deep stretching and to improve circulation in the joints. Yang yoga, in contrast, is the type of yoga that people often practice for exercise and to build strength and improve cardiac function. The deep stretching that occurs in restorative yoga practice has a profound calming effect on the nervous system.

1. Read through these instructions before beginning. You may also wish to look at photographs of these poses on my website, AMindfulMD.com.

2. A yoga mat will be helpful. Yin yoga can be even more restorative with the support of blankets and pillows, so have these handy.

3. Sit on your mat, stretch your legs out in front of you, and spread them as far apart as is comfortable. Inhale and reach your arms up to the sky. On your exhale, fold forward at your hips and reach your arms toward the floor in between your legs; this is the yoga pose seated split-leg forward fold. You may rest your forehead on a pillow or blankets. Stay here and breathe for several minutes.

4. Come to lying on your back and have your pillows and your blankets nearby. You may wish to have a pillow under your head and/or lower back for more support. Bend your knees, spread them wide, and bring the soles of your feet together to touch; this is reclined bound angle pose. You may wish to place pillows under your knees for support. You can rest your arms along

your sides or perhaps bring them over your head for a shoulder stretch. Feel free to cover yourself with a blanket. Stay in this pose and breathe for several minutes. When you are ready to move on to the next pose, slowly straighten your legs long and return to lying on your back.

5. Flip over so you are lying on your belly with your legs together. Bend your right knee at a 90-degree angle, which will open your right hip, and slide your bent knee up along the mat until it is in line with your hip. Extend your right arm to make an L on the mat, with your elbow in line with your shoulder and bent at a 90-degree angle. This is prone half frog on your right side. Breathe here for a couple of minutes and then repeat on your left side.

6. End your practice in savasana pose: lie on your back with your legs extended, feet apart, and toes turned out. Angle your arms evenly away from the sides of your body with your palms facing up.

Nurture Your Nervous System: If you struggle with anxiety, I recommend that you practice restorative yoga at least once a week, because it builds more parasympathetic tone that will help you regulate your reactivity. You may wish to dim the lights, play calm music, and use aromatherapy during your practice. You can also look for restorative yoga videos or classes.

Living with Higher Purpose and Releasing Attachments

10 minutes

A powerful way to cultivate stillness is to live your life in deep alignment with your values and release attachments to things that are beyond your control. When you focus on your intentions and live with integrity, so many of your concerns and preoccupations drop away. You become confident that you are truly doing the best you can, and you commit to letting go of all the external factors you cannot control.

1. Find a quiet place to write and reflect on the following prompts.

2. What values are important to you? Consider this list of values and add any others you think of that are important to you: honesty, justice, equality, temperance, prudence, compassion, non-violence, fidelity, trust, discipline, responsibility, commitment, courage, respect, hard work, loyalty, learning, reflection, achievement, collaboration, humility, cleanliness, security. Which values are most important to you?

3. In what way(s) are you not living in accordance with the values that are important to you? What areas would you like to work on? Can you commit to any small steps that you can begin to incorporate into your daily life?

4. The Buddha taught the Noble Eightfold Path as the way to end suffering. The eight steps on that path are Right Understanding, Right Thought, Right Speech, Right Action, Right Livelihood, Right Effort, Right Mindfulness, and Right Concentration. This is another lens through which you can reflect on both your internal and your

external practices and become clear on where there is potential for growth. Would you like to focus on any of these eight? Can you set any small goals that you can begin to work toward?

5. You can reflect and work toward living more in alignment with your values, but there are many variables that are outside of your control, including the outcome of your actions, how other people react and behave, and other external conditions. For example, when you go on a job interview, you can do your best, but ultimately the outcome is out of your hands. You are wise to focus on setting strong intentions, living in accordance with your values, and letting go of any attachments to a particular outcome. Do you have difficulty letting go of attachments to outcomes, other peoples' thoughts, feelings, or actions, or other variables outside of your control?

Right Understanding: You can spend a lot of time focusing on how other people feel about you or treat you because you mistakenly believe that this is somehow a reflection of who you are. Other peoples' feelings and actions are actually much more a reflection of who they are. Empower yourself by focusing on *your* thoughts, feelings, and actions.

Balancing Growth and Acceptance

15 minutes

There is a fine balance between continuing to grow and accepting and loving yourself right now. As you work toward growth in your stillness practice (as well as in many other areas of your life), you may have a tendency to emphasize growth at the expense of self-love and self-acceptance. You can become so focused on becoming "better" that you are unable to see all the beauty inside yourself right here and now.

1. Find a quiet place to write and reflect on the following prompts.

2. Do you have difficulty feeling good about yourself, just as you are right here and now? Do you find that you often feel as if you need to become better or stronger in some areas of your life to be okay? Is it difficult to rest when you need to? Do you tend to tie up your worth in your accomplishments? Some people received a lot of love, praise, and/or acknowledgment for achievements as children, but unfortunately, unconditional love may have not been communicated. Did you receive the message as a child that your worth was tied up in your accomplishments? How so?

3. You are exactly where you need to be right here and right now. This is your path. Growth is awesome, but you do not need it to be okay. Your worth is unconditional. Do you believe this? If not, why not?

4. Many people are afraid that if they love or accept themselves, they may become passive or lazy in their lives. This practice is about more balance. People who tend to be very driven are likely not going to become

couch potatoes. Drive is a spectrum, and you can aim to move even just a small bit closer to self-love and self-acceptance.

5. Some people believe that thinking they are in some way lacking or deficient is good motivation for continued growth. Do you have this belief? Operating with this belief works against you, though, because it erodes your confidence in and acceptance of yourself. If you work toward unconditional self-love and acceptance, you will find you have a much easier time accomplishing your goals.

6. Can you give yourself the unconditional love that you may not have received as a child?

Resting: Changing your behaviors can help you adjust your underlying beliefs. Practice resting more, even if you feel the impulse to be constantly doing and achieving. This may be uncomfortable at first, but if you stick with it, you will begin to see the benefit of resting and realize that you are okay just being.

Accepting Impermanence

Everything in life is impermanent. We are often fooled into believing that our thoughts, feelings, moods, circumstances, and even our bodies and lives have some unchanging nature that will go on forever, but they don't; all of life is always shifting and changing. Believing that reality is static is a frequent cause of confusion that leads to much suffering. Here, you will explore your beliefs around impermanence and look at how this concept manifests in your life.

1. Find a quiet place to write and reflect on the following prompts.

2. When you are feeling down, overwhelmed, or particularly upset, how often do you believe these feelings will be with you forever? When you believe this, does it help? How would your experiences be different if you could instead remember that all feelings are temporary and you practice showing up for yourself with self-compassion when you are not feeling well?

3. On the flip side, do you find yourself trying to cling to your good feelings and the good times in your life, not wanting them to end? Although this may be a more subtle form of suffering, it also contributes to your inner discontent and turmoil. Imagine you are a leaf floating down a river, and let the current of life guide your journey.

4. Life often doesn't go as planned, but if you look, you can find beauty nonetheless. Have there been big changes in your life, some of which may have been quite difficult? One very difficult change is when people we love

pass away, leave, or change in challenging ways. Even though your life may not be as you planned, can you appreciate the beauty in it right now?

5. As you become older and deal with illness or other limitations, you may struggle. Have you dealt with any of this? Do you have any underlying resistant beliefs around aging and/or illness that may make these transitions more difficult? Can you release any of this resistance?

6. Reflecting on your mortality can provide a lot of perspective and clarity. When difficult situations are happening in your life, asking yourself whether they will matter in one, five, or ten years, or on your deathbed, can provide much-needed perspective. What is something that has been stressing you out lately? How do you believe you will feel about this at the very end of your life?

Gaining Perspective: Knowing that your time here on this planet with your loved ones is limited can also help you be grateful for all you have and spend your time in meaningful ways. If you knew that you only had a week left to live, how would you live differently?

Moving Forward in Peace

Congratulations on finishing this book and coming to the end of this part of your stillness journey. Thank yourself for carving out this time to invest in your health and well-being. Pause and reflect on all the benefits you have accrued from your time, commitment, and practice. The wisdom and skills you developed will serve you and those around you well. We have such a strong tendency to dwell in the past and live for the future, so your ability to ground yourself and enjoy where you are right now is so important for your peace.

As this part of your journey ends, there will be many opportunities ahead to deepen your stillness practice. Please check out the resources and references in the next sections for some ideas. There are so many amazing books, podcasts, classes, and guided meditations available. You may wish to find an in-person or online community that will support you on your continued journey.

If any particular practices resonated with you, please continue to practice them regularly, trying to lengthen the time that you stay in stillness practice. You may wish to look for spiritual teachers you can work with directly or spiritually informed psychotherapists; I strongly recommend doing this, particularly if you have a history of trauma or if any of the practices brought up feelings that felt overwhelming.

This stillness work you do is so important. Thank you for adding peace to our world.

Resources

Aha! Parenting (AhaParenting.com)
Dr. Laura Markham, a clinical psychologist and mom, teaches and writes about peaceful parenting, a relationship-based parenting model which incorporates a number of stillness practices and principles and is based on the latest child-development research.

Eckhart Tolle (EckhartTolle.com)
Eckhart Tolle is a powerful spiritual teacher and author. His book *The Power of Now* can be transformative.

Insight Meditation Society (Dharma.org/resources/meditation-centers-and-communities)
Insight Meditation Society is one of the oldest meditation centers in the West and was cofounded by Sharon Salzberg, Joseph Goldstein, and Jack Kornfield in 1976. This link has a list of insight centers across the world.

Jack Kornfield (JackKornfield.com)
Jack Kornfield is another favorite spiritual teacher and author who is also a psychologist. His website has a lot of information on his books, podcasts, and retreats.

Pema Chodron (PemaChodronFoundation.org)
Pema Chodron is a Buddhist teacher and author who writes beautifully about finding peace during difficult times.

Plum Village (PlumVillage.org)
Plum Village is a global community founded by Zen Master Thich Nhat Hanh, who published more than 100 books and was also a peace activist. Thich Nhat Hanh passed away January 22, 2022, and his death was felt around the world. There are Plum Village gatherings, called sanghas, in many neighborhoods, and the website includes a list of them.

Ram Dass (RamDass.org)
Ram Dass was a powerful spiritual teacher and author who passed away in 2019. His students maintain a site about his teachings.

Sharon Salzberg (SharonSalzberg.com)
Sharon Salzberg is one of my favorite spiritual teachers and authors. Her website has a lot of information on her books, podcasts, and other offerings.

Tara Brach (TaraBrach.com)
Tara Brach is a spiritual teacher, author, and psychologist. Her website has a lot of information on her books, podcasts, and courses.

The Untethered Soul (UntetheredSoul.com)
Michael Singer wrote *The Untethered Soul,* a powerful spiritual book that helps readers free themselves from habitual thoughts and emotions.

The Work of Byron Katie (TheWork.com)
Byron Katie developed the Work, which is a simple but transformative spiritual tool that includes meditation and self-inquiry. She has written several books that many people find to be powerful.

Yoga Journal (YogaJournal.com)
Yoga Journal's website has a comprehensive searchable database of yoga poses, with photos and helpful tips for doing them. There's also a helpful section on meditation.

References

Chin, F., R. Chou, M. Waqas, K. Vakharia, H. Rai, E. Levy, and D. Holmes. "Efficacy of Prayer in Inducing Immediate Physiological Changes: A Systematic Analysis of Objective Experiments." *Journal of Complementary and Integrative Medicine* 18, no. 4 (2021): 679–84. doi: 10.1515/jcim-2020-0075.

Cocchiara, R. A., M. Peruzzo, A. Mannocci, L. Ottolenghi, P. Villari, A. Polimeni, F. Guerra, and G. La Torre. "The Use of Yoga to Manage Stress and Burnout in Healthcare Workers: A Systematic Review." *Journal of Clinical Medicine* 8, no. 3 (2019): 284. doi: 10.3390/jcm8030284.

Danhauer, S. C., E. L. Addington, S. J. Sohl, A. Chaoul, and L. Cohen. "Review of Yoga Therapy during Cancer Treatment." *Supportive Care in Cancer* 25, no. 4 (2017): 1357–72. doi: 10.1007/s00520-016-3556-9.

Della Valle, E., S. Palermi, I. Aloe, R. Marcantonio, R. Spera, S. Montagnani, and F. Sirico. "Effectiveness of Workplace Yoga Interventions to Reduce Perceived Stress in Employees: A Systematic Review and Meta-Analysis." *Journal of Functional Morphology and Kinesiology* 5, no. 2 (2020): 33. doi: 10.3390/jfmk5020033.

de Vibe, M., I. Solhaug, R. Tyssen, O. Friborg, J. H. Rosenvinge, T. Sørlie, and A. Bjørndal. "Mindfulness Training for Stress Management: A Randomised Controlled Study of Medical and Psychology Students." *BMC Medical Education* 13 (2013): 107. doi: 10.1186/1472-6920-13-107.

Dunning, D. L., K. Griffiths, W. Kuyken, C. Crane, L. Foulkes, J. Parker, and T. Dalgleish. "Research Review: The Effects of Mindfulness-Based Interventions on Cognition and Mental

Health in Children and Adolescents—A Meta-Analysis of Randomized Controlled Trials." *Journal of Child Psychology and Psychiatry* 60, no. 3 (2019): 244–58. doi: 10.1111 /jcpp.12980.

Gallegos, A. M., H. F. Crean, W. R. Pigeon, and K. L. Heffner. "Meditation and Yoga for Posttraumatic Stress Disorder: A Meta-Analytic Review of Randomized Controlled Trials." *Clinical Psychology Review* 58 (2017): 115–24. doi: 10.1016 /j.cpr.2017.10.004.

Greeson, J. M., and G. R. Chin. "Mindfulness and Physical Disease: A Concise Review." *Current Opinion in Psychology* 28 (2019): 204–10. doi: 10.1016/j.copsyc.2018.12.014.

Janssen, M., Y. Heerkens, W. Kuijer, B. van der Heijden, and J. Engels. "Effects of Mindfulness-Based Stress Reduction on Employees' Mental Health: A Systematic Review." *PLoS One* 13, no. 1 (2018): e0191332. doi: 10.1371/journal.pone.0191332.

Kawanishi, Y., S. J. B. Hanley, K. Tabata, Y. Nakagi, T. Ito, E. Yoshioka, T. Yoshida, and Y. Saijo. "Effects of Prenatal Yoga: A Systematic Review of Randomized Controlled Trials." [In Japanese.] *Nihon Koshu Eisei* Zasshi [Japanese journal of public health] 62, no. 5 (2015): 221-31. doi: 10.11236 /jph.62.5_221. English abstract at PubMed.NCBI.NLM.NIH .gov/26118705.

Kiran, A. K. A., D. Kaur, and R. Ghay. "Impact of Meditation on Autonomic Nervous System—A Research Study." *International Journal of Basic and Applied Medical Sciences.* 1, no. 1 (2011): 144–48. CIBTech.org/J-MEDICAL-SCIENCES /PUBLICATIONS/2011/Vol%201%20No.%201/58-23-jls -kiran.pdf.

Lawrence, M., F. T. Celestino Junior, H. H. S. Matozinho, L. Govan, J. Booth, and J. Beecher. "Yoga for Stroke Rehabilitation." *Cochrane Database of Systematic Reviews*, no. 12 (2017): CD011483. doi: 10.1002/14651858.CD011483.pub2.

Lemay, V., J. Hoolahan, and A. Buchanan. "Impact of a Yoga and Meditation Intervention on Students' Stress and Anxiety Levels." *American Journal of Pharmaceutical Education* 83, no. 5 (2019): 7001. doi: 10.5688/ajpe7001.

O'Reilly, G. A., L. Cook, D. Spruijt-Metz, and D. S. Black. "Mindfulness-Based Interventions for Obesity-Related Eating Behaviours: A Literature Review" *Obesity Reviews* 15, no. 6 (2014): 453-61. doi: 10.1111/obr.12156.

Saeed, S. A., K. Cunningham, and R. M. Bloch. "Depression and Anxiety Disorders: Benefits of Exercise, Yoga, and Meditation." *American Family Physician* 99, no. 10 (2019): 620–27. AAFP .org/afp/2019/0515/p620.html.

Schuman-Olivier, Z., M. Trombka, D. A. Lovas, J. A. Brewer, D. R. Vago, R. Gawande, J. P. Dunne, S. W. Lazar, E. B. Loucks, and C. Fulwiler. "Mindfulness and Behavior Change." *Harvard Review of Psychiatry* 28, no. 6 (2020): 371–94. doi: 10.1097 /HRP.0000000000000277.

Thind, H., R. Lantini, B. L. Balletto, M. L. Donahue, E. Salmoraigo -Blotcher, B. C. Bock, and L. A. J. Scott-Sheldon. "The Effects of Yoga among Adults with Type 2 Diabetes: A Systematic Review and Meta-Analysis." *Preventive Medicine* 105 (2017): 116–26. doi: 10.1016/j.ypmed.2017.08.017.

Tyagi, A., and M. Cohen. "Yoga and Heart Rate Variability: A Comprehensive Review of the Literature." *International Journal of Yoga* 9, no. 2 (2016): 97-113. doi: 10.4103/0973-6131.183712.

Wieland, L. S., N. Skoetz, K. Pilkington, R. Vempati, C. R. D'Adamo, and B. M. Berman. "Yoga Treatment for Chronic Non-Specific Low Back Pain." *Cochrane Database of Systematic Reviews*, no. 1 (2017): CD010671. doi: 10.1002/14651858.CD010671.pub2.

Wielgosz, J., S. B. Goldberg, T. R. A. Kral, J. D. Dunne, and R. J. Davidson. "Mindfulness Meditation and Psychopathology." *Annual Review of Clinical Psychology* 15 (2019): 285-316. doi: 10.1146/annurev-clinpsy-021815-093423.

Yang, Z.-Y., H.-B. Zhong, C. Mao, J.-Q. Yuan, Y. Huang, X.-Y. Wu, Y.-M. Gao, and J.-L. Tang. "Yoga for Asthma." *Cochrane Database of Systematic Reviews*, no. 4 (2016): CD010346. doi: 10.1002/14651858.CD010346.pub2.

Zeidan, F., and D. R. Vago. "Mindfulness Meditation–Based Pain Relief: A Mechanistic Account." *Annals of the New York Academy of Sciences* 1373, no. 1 (2016): 114-27. doi: 10.1111/nyas.13153.

Zhang, M.-F., Y.-S. Wen, W.-Y. Liu, L.-F. Peng, X.-D. Wu, and Q.-W. Liu. "Effectiveness of Mindfulness-Based Therapy for Reducing Anxiety and Depression in Patients With Cancer: A Meta-Analysis." *Medicine* 94, no. 45 (2015): e0897-0. doi: 10.1097/MD.0000000000000897.

Index

A

Acceptance
  about, 18
  balancing growth
      and, 126–127
  of impermanence, 128–129
Anger, awareness of, 88–89
Anxiety, 11
Attachments, releasing,
      and living with higher
      purpose, 124–125
Aversion, awareness
      of, 64–65
Awareness
  of anger, 88–89
  of aversion, 64–65
  of confusion, 72–73
  of craving, 68–69
  of ego, 60–61
  of emotions, 58–59
  of fear, 84–85
  of interdependence, 118–119
  open, 116–117
  of sadness, 92–93
  of sense perceptions, 32–33
  of thoughts, 44–45

B

Balancing postures, 104–105
Bathing, mindful, 62–63
Beginner's mind, 24–25, 77
Body scan, 38–39
Body tension, releasing, 54–55

Breathwork

Breathwork
  about, 23
  calm breathing, 36–37
  mindfulness of the
      breath, 30–31
Buddhism, 4

C

Calm breathing, 36–37
Children, stillness with, 94–95
Christianity, 5
Conflict, practicing with, 114–115
Confusion, awareness of, 72–73
Contentment, cultivating, 120–121
Craving, awareness of, 68–69

D

Depression, 12

E

Eating in stillness, 52–53
Ego, awareness of, 60–61
Emails, stillness before
      responding to, 74–75
Embracing your inner child, 96–97
Emotions
  awareness of, 58–59
  self-compassion with
      difficult, 78–79

F

Fear, awareness of, 84–85
Forgiveness practice, 110–111

G

Gratitude practice, 98–99
Growth and acceptance,
    balancing, 126–127

H

Head and neck tension,
    releasing, 46–47
Higher purpose, living
    with, and releasing
    attachments, 124–125
Hip opening, 108–109
Household chores,
    mindfulness in, 76–77

I

Impermanence, accepting, 128–129
Inner child, embracing your, 96–97
Intention setting, 19
Interdependence, awareness
    of, 118–119

J

Journaling, 48–49
Judgment. See Non-judging

K

Kabat-Zinn, Jon, 11

L

Letting go, 16–17
Living with higher purpose and
    releasing attachments, 124–125
Love, moving in the direction
    of, 112–113
Loving-kindness meditation,
    42–43, 89
    street loving-kindness, 82–83

M

Media reflection, 106–107
Meditation
    about, 23
    loving-kindness, 42–43, 89
    street loving-kindness, 82–83
    sun salutation, 90–91
    walking, 40–41
Mindfulness
    about, 5–6
    in bathing, 62–63
    of the breath, 30–31
    in household chores, 76–77
    in morning routines, 56–57
    in movement, 34–35
    principles of, 15–18, 50–51
Mindfulness-based stress
    reduction (MBSR), 11
Morning routine, mindful, 56–57
Movement, mindful, 34–35

N

Noise of technology, 8–9
Non-judging, 16
Non-striving, 17

O

Open awareness, 116–117

P

Patience, 17
Physical health, benefits to, 10
Present moment grounding, 20

R

Relationships, stillness in, 80–81
Restorative yoga, 122–123

S

Sadness, awareness of, 92–93
Self-compassion with difficult
  emotions, 78–79
Sense perceptions,
  awareness of, 32–33
Shopping, stillness in, 100–101
Sleep, stillness before, 66–67
Spine, warming up the, 70–71
Stillness
  aspects of, 15–18
  benefits of, 9–12
  history of, 3–6
  meaning of, 7–8
  in modern times, 6–7
  overview, 13, 26
  as a practice, 18–23, 131
Stillness practices
  with children, 94–95
  eating, 52–53
  on the go, 86–87
  in relationships, 80–81
  before responding to
    emails, 74–75
  in shopping, 100–101
  before sleep, 66–67
Stoicism, 4–5
Stress, 11
Sun salutation, 90–91

T

Technology, noise of, 8–9
  media reflection, 106–107
  stillness before responding to
    emails, 74–75
Tension
  releasing in the body, 54–55
  releasing in the head and
    neck, 46–47
Thoughts, awareness of, 44–45
Trust, 17–18

V

Visualization, 24

W

Walking meditation, 40–41
Well-being, benefits to, 10
Work-life balance, 102–103

Y

Yoga
  about, 4
  balancing postures, 104–105
  hip opening, 108–109
  mindful movement, 34–35
  restorative, 122–123
  sun salutation, 90–91
  warming up the spine, 70–71

Acknowledgments

I would like to thank my partner, my family, and my therapists for all their love and support throughout my many life endeavors. I am grateful to all my spiritual teachers who have taught me to be more present and loving. A special thanks to J. Greg Serpa, PhD, for sharing all your love and knowledge of mindfulness with me. Finally, thank you to all my patients for the inspiring and nourishing work that we do together.

About the Author

 **Nissa Keyashian**, MD, is a board-certified psychiatrist and also blogs at AMindfulMD.com about emotional, physical, and spiritual health. She lives with her partner and her two sons in San Jose, California.